DROP
US A
LINE...

SUCKER!

DROP US A LINE...

SUCKER!

The Prank Letters of James and Stuart Wade

Carroll & Graf Publishers, Inc.
New York

First edition July 1995.

Front cover designed and copyrighted © 1995 by Archie Ferguson

Carroll & Graf Publishers
260 Fifth Avenue
New York, NY 10001

Library of Congress Cataloging-in-Publication Data

  Wade, James C.
  Drop us a line— sucker! : the prank letters of James and
    Stuart Wade. — 1st ed.
          p.   cm.
  ISBN 0-7867-0205-2 (trade paper)
  1. Letters—Humor. 2. Wit and humor. 3. American wit and humor.
    I. Wade, Stuart. II. Title
  PN6131.W33   1995
  818'.5407—dc20   95-7743
                                          CIP

Manufactured in the United States of America.

5   4   3   2

TO

Christi, Rosine, Cynthia, Claire, Virginia, Kara, Françoise, Jeanie, Lisa, Sylvie, Lucretia, Cricket, Gretchen, and especially Sue, with lots of love.

INTRODUCTION

At Indiana University there is a special word used to describe an elaborate practical joke: it's called a "borass." Nobody seems to know where this term comes from—we've never seen it in any dictionary—but it goes back at least to the 1920s, since our two grandfathers, and especially our dad, all I.U. alums, loved to recount borasses of theirs which over the years had become the stuff of legend (well, at least to *them*.)

By the time the two of us were in college, "borassing" had gone beyond pranksterism to become an art form, especially in our fraternity (which shall go nameless to protect the not-so-innocent). Alongside some true masters, we rolled up our sleeves and did our part for the legends of tomorrow. But with borassing already in our blood, can our predeliction for pranks be chalked up to *nature or nurture?* Hard to say. We would guess a combination of factors are at work. If we hadn't had Jim Wade as our dad, and the "men of Beechwood" as coaches and mentors, writing this book would have been unthinkable.

Jav and **WSW**

DROP US A LINE...

SUCKER!

JAMES C. WADE III

P.O. Box 103
Montchoisi
1000 Lausanne 19
Switzerland

May 20th, 1992

Listerine Product Manager
Warner Lambert Corporation
Lambert Court,
Chestnut Avenue,
GB-Eastleigh, Hampshire, SO5 3ZQ
England

Dear sir or madam,

I was at a dinner party recently at which the most delicious hors-d'oeuvres were served which I have ever eaten. Imagine my surprise when the hostess told me they were Listerine balls! Round and chewy and with the taste of Listerine, only more cheese-like.

She told me that I could write to Listerine for a pamphlet containing all kinds of recipes for dishes made with Listerine, including an exquisite Hollandaise sauce. Could you please send me a copy?

Thank you very much in advance. Looking forward to hearing from you, I am

Yours sincerely,

2

LISTERINE
Antiseptic Mouthwash

Please quote reference in all correspondence
Ref: CM8/45(2)

14 July 1992

Mr. James C. Wade III,
PO Box 103,
Montchoisi,
1000 Lausanne 19,
SWITZERLAND

Dear Mr. Wade III,

Thank you for your letter regarding our product Listerine.

Listerine has been formulated for use as an antiseptic mouthwash which helps to freshen breath and reduce the build up of plaque.

I am afraid that there has been some misunderstanding, unless of course, there is a swiss product suitable for cooking which has the same name.

Thank you for taking the time and trouble to write.

Yours sincerely,

Sharon Simmonds

Sharon Simmonds
CONSUMER ADVISORY BUREAU

Clifford

**WARNER
LAMBERT
HEALTH CARE**

Lambert Court, Chestnut Avenue,
Eastleigh, Hampshire SO5 3ZQ.

Listerine is a trade mark.

3

W. STUART WADE

3023 N. Clark Street, No. 789
Chicago, Illinois 60657

January 5th, 1993

Manager, Time and Temperature Line
c/o Superior Systems, Inc.
P.O. Box 211
Livonia, Michigan 48154

Re: Unsolicited information

Dear sirs,

I live in Chicago which I have learned uses your company's service to provide the "Time and Temperature" recording when you dial 976.

Over the years I suppose I have called 976 a few dozen times, always without a problem. Since a few weeks ago, however, your service has become a major irritant. For some reason, Time and Temperature keeps calling *me*. I cannot tell you how annoying it is to get calls at all hours of the day and night which are nothing more than a cheery recorded voice saying, "It's 18 degrees at 2:21!" This is driving me around the bend.

My previous complaints have gone unheeded. Meanwhile I am losing sleep and ruining my health answering the phone in the middle of the night.

Frankly, I really don't understand why you are unable to control your recording any better than this and at this point, I insist that you correct the situation at once. If you cannot resolve this problem immediately, I see little alternative but for me to turn to certain people in a position of power (Illinois Bell, Oprah Winfrey, etc.) to get things done. I am sure that you would like to avoid the glare and attention of the media if at all possible.

Sincerely yours,

W. Stuart Wade

AUDIOTEX SERVICES INC.

600 South Federal Street, Suite 122
Chicago, Illinois 60605
312/906-3130
Fax: 312/906-3110
800-432-0080

January 11, 1992

Mr. W. Stuart Wade
3023 North Clark Street, #789
Chicago, IL 60657

Dear Mr. Wade:

Superior Systems uses our equipment for their 976 programs in Chicago, and Mr. Oliver Masys of Superior Systems, Inc. has asked me to respond to your attached letter.

I can attest to the fact that the annoying calls you have experienced are not from any of the programs using our equipment. These services are not programmed to generate outbound calls. However, it is conceivable that other 976 programs such as wake up services may be involved. Ameritech Audiotex Services does not provide any such wake up services, but I offer to assist you in your efforts to get this issue resolved.

Please contact me at 312-906-3118. I hope to hear from you.

Sincerely,

Brian Eaton
Project Manager

fax copy to: O.Masys, Superior Systems

W. STUART WADE

3023 N. Clark Street, No. 789
Chicago, Illinois 60657

January 26th, 1993

Mr. Brian Eaton
Project Manager, Time and Temperature
Ameritech Audiotex Services Inc.
600 South Federal Street, Suite 122
Chicago, Illinois 60605

Dear Mr. Eaton,

Thank you for your letter of January 11th. I am sorry I didn't respond earlier, but on the 14th I simply moved out of my apartment as I could no longer stand the constant ringing. Yesterday I came in to pick up the mail and found your letter. I immediately tried phoning you, but the only response I got at the number you gave me was "the date line."

To bring you up to speed on the situation: from about the 8th of January onward, Time and Temperature called me every half hour, day and night. Oddly enough, I noticed that the recorded time started gradually falling behind the real time, at first by just a few minutes but eventually it was about six hours behind. I believe the temperature readings may have been off, too, as I don't recall any day in the past two weeks when it has been in the high 80's. Once or twice I could swear the recorded voice was chuckling.

When I arrived to pick up my mail yesterday, I was met at the door by your work crew, who somehow solved the problem. Your foreman explained that once a 976 program "locks on" a number, the only way to fix it is by rerouting the calls to Wisconsin Bell and basically passing the problem on to someone up there. Whatever works is fine by me, but I wish you could have tried this earlier. At any rate, everything is back to normal again. I assume these calls won't show up on my bill.

Thank you for your help, and please pass on my thanks to your foreman, Mr. Don Shirley.

Sincerely,

W. Stuart Wade

AMERITECH

AUDIOTEX SERVICES INC.

January 29, 1993

600 South Federal Street
Suite 122
Chicago, Illinois 60605
Voice: 312/906-3130
Fax: 312/906-3110
800-432-0080

Mr. W. Stuart Wade
3023 North Clark Street
Chicago, IL 60657

Dear Mr. Wade:

Your recent letter (dated Jan. 26, 1993) responding to my letter to you contains inaccurate information.

First, the only number referenced in my letter to you was the direct line to my office. It is <u>not</u> likely that you reached "the date line" when calling my number - unless the number was incorrectly dialed.

Second, Ameritech Audiotex Services did <u>not</u> send a work crew to your location, and Mr. Don Shirley does <u>not</u> work for us. I do not understand the explanation given to you, but I am pleased to hear that the problem has since been corrected.

Although this situation clearly is <u>not</u> associated with Ameritech Audiotex Services, you are free to contact me with questions or for assistance. If these calls appear on your bill, I suggest that you contact an Illinois Bell Telephone representative at 800-244-4444 for assistance.

Sincerely,

Brian Eaton

Brian Eaton

7

JAMES C. WADE III

P.O. Box 103
Montchoisi
1000 Lausanne 19
Switzerland

December 29th, 1992

Colorado State Fair
Attn. Organizing Committee
c/o Colorado State Fairgrounds
Pueblo, Colorado 81004
USA

Dear sirs,

Some very disturbing news concerning your 1993 State Fair has come across my desk recently. It was my original intention to pass this information directly to Dr. Frazier Butthope at Speak Up (the Global Foundation for the Protection of Dumb Animals), but in fairness to you, I will not take this step without first hearing what you have to say.

Can you please confirm whether it is true that in next year's rodeo, the cowboys will be allowed to use flame throwers to control the broncos? Apart from being pointless and mean, may I remind you that this would violate Section 8, Paragraph 17(b) of the Geneva Convention and would land your organization in some very hot water.

I look forward to receiving a timely response.

Yours sincerely,

8

February 22, 1993

Mr. James C. Wade III
P.O. Box 103
1000 Lausanne 19
Switzerland

Dear Mr. Wade:

In response to your letter concerning flame throwers to control broncos,
I can hardly imagine anything further for the truth then this outrageous
idea.

I can assure you number one, that flame throwers are not here on the
Colorado State Fairgrounds and they are in no way a part of the sport
of rodeo.

Sincerely,

Jerry Robbe,
President/General Manager

JR/jp

W. STUART WADE

3023 N. Clark Street, No. 789
Chicago, Illinois 60657

September 26th, 1992

Shulton, Inc.
Attn: Product Manager, Old Spice Stick Deodorant
Wayne, New Jersey 07470

Dear sir or madam,

I have a serious problem with your product, and I hope you will be able to help me solve it.

For at least ten years, I have been a user of Old Spice stick deodorants. I have always considered it the best deodorant on the market (in fact I still do.)

A couple of years ago, I began to notice that after applying Old Spice under my arms, I would experience a strange, yet very positive feeling. It is difficult to put into words, but it was a nice, soothing sensation which I felt not only under my arms, but all over. Because it made me feel so good, I began to reapply Old Spice at lunchtime at the office and again before going to bed. Within a few months, I was dashing into the men's room at work six or seven times a day to put on more Old Spice, sometimes without even realizing it. As you can imagine, people at work began to talk.

Somehow this has gotten out of hand. I am now applying Old Spice 20 or 30 times a day, and I feel sure that something must be wrong with me, or with the product. If I don't apply Old Spice first thing in the morning, I get nervous flutters and can't eat breakfast. But as soon as I put it on, I calm down and eventually (after several strokes) reach the euphoric feeling I described before. It gives me a clearheaded feeling of power and invincibility.

I once tried to switch to another brand, but I became irritable and after two days I could not stop my arms from twitching. Is it possible that I have become addicted to Old Spice? What is in that stuff? Please help me—I cannot understand what is happening.

Sincerely yours,

W. Stuart Wade

PS. I once switched from "Fresh Scent" to "Island Breeze" but I just got headaches.

Procter&Gamble

The Procter & Gamble Company
Public Affairs Division
P.O. Box 599, Cincinnati, Ohio 45201-0599

October 30, 1992

MR W STUART WADE
3023 N CLARK ST #789
CHICAGO IL 60657

Dear Mr. Wade:

Thank you for writing about Old Spice Stick Deodorant.

It is hard to know whether there is some hidden medical condition
that is provoking your strange reaction to Old Spice Stick Deodorant.
It certainly would be quite unusual, but one which you would have to
work out with your physician after a thorough evaluation.

Thanks again for writing.

Sincerely,

Ellen Voellger

Ellen Voellger
Consumer Services

EV:pw

11

JAMES C. WADE III

P.O. Box 103
Montchoisi
1000 Lausanne 19
Switzerland

July 3rd, 1992

The Rector,
Winchester Cathedral
Winchester, Hants. SO23 9LS
England

Dear sir,

I would like to know if the Cathedral might be used in November of this year to hold a requiem in honor of Mr. P. Castor Mahoney, a very dear friend who passed away last month in Lapland, another tragic victim of reindeer-transmitted brucellosis (RTB).

Castor had friends all over the world, many of whom will certainly come to a memorial service if we give them ample time to make travel arrangements. Therefore I believe we need a large church; I thought of holding the service in Winchester Cathedral since this was Castor's favorite song.

If etiquette permits, I would like to include as many of these friends as possible in the service itself. Of course, not everyone will be able to take an active role, but it is gratifying that so many of his admirers have already asked if they can do something special in his remembrance.

Would you see any problem if the 17th Regiment of the Nigerian Presidential Rifles were to perform some close-order drill in the nave of the Cathedral? (This is the unit under Col. Eleven Mkembe-Jones, whom you may know.) The Colonel assures me that all their firearms will be registered with Customs, and if you would prefer, I'm sure they could forgo fixing bayonets. As for the chanting of the traditional "Nkwekwe," Mkembe-Jones has told me in all candor that it can turn rather grim. I don't think you need worry, however, as his men are doubtless well disciplined, and I feel certain the Colonel would not tolerate any ritual bloodshed.

Of course it goes without saying that we would like to make a generous donation to the upkeep of the Cathedral, or to an appropriate charity, to thank you for making such a service possible.

I look forward to hearing from you soon, and thank you very kindly for taking the time to consider this private and still rather painful matter.

Yours sincerely,

[signature]

12

JAMES C. WADE III

P.O. Box 103
Montchoisi
1000 Lausanne 19
Switzerland

July 4th, 1992

The Rector,
Winchester Cathedral
Winchester, Hants.
England

<u>Re: Mr. P. Castor Mahoney, Memorial Service, November</u>

Dear sir,

Following my letter dated yesterday, I have received this morning a note from Mrs. Arlene Lomax of the Simian Fund for Human Development, who heard that I was trying to organize a service and would very much like to take part.

Mrs. Lomax writes that she would be prepared to sing five or six songs which will remind us all of Castor in his happier days at the Orang-Utan Club. Could you please ask your organist if he knows "Rubber Band Man" by the O'Jays? If he doesn't know that one, Mrs. Lomax mentions that another favorite of Castor's was "Boogie Oogie Oogie."

I am sure that there will be many such details to discuss as we go forward with our plans, but I wanted to check this particular question with you now, since Mrs. Lomax says she needs several weeks to train her dogs.

Looking forward to your response, I remain

Sincerely yours,

James Wade

PS. Does your Choir Director happen to have any sheet music from "Oklahoma!"?

WINCHESTER CATHEDRAL

The Dean of Winchester

The Deanery Winchester SO23 9LS
Telephone (0962) 853738

Mr James C Wade III   22 July 1992
P O Box 103
Montchoisi
1000 Lausanne 19
Switzerland

Dear Mr Wade,

I thank you for your letter of 3rd July.

While it would be a great honour for us to arrange a Memorial
Service for the late Mr P Castor Mahoney who died so tragically
in Lapland, I am afraid that we must decline your request.

Although Winchester Cathedral is the second longest church in
the world, after St Peter's Rome, it would I fear not be large
enough for the great numbers of Mr Mahoney's admirers who would
wish to attend, neither would there be sufficient space for the
advanced liturgical activities you have in mind.

Clearly, no other church in Winchester would be suitable for your
purpose, so I suggest that you now approach His Holiness the Pope
to see if the service might be held in St Peter's. This would
have several advantages besides the size of the great basilica.

The journey for the 17th Regiment of the Nigerian Presidential
Rifles would be significantly shorter and the weather in Rome
in November would certainly be more agreeable than it is likely
to be in Winchester where we may well have dense fog. The presence
of the Pope would obviously add a special touch of splendour to
the occasion.

There is the further point that the Vatican's finances are in
a parlous state and it seems appropriate that your generous donation
should go where it is most needed.

I hope you may find these suggestions helpful and that the great
Memorial Service in November will help assuage the personal pain
which, inevitably, you are now feeling.

Yours sincerely,

14

W. STUART WADE

3023 N. Clark Street, Box 789
Chicago, Illinois 60657

July 20th, 1992

The Ralston Purina Co.
Attn. Manager, Dog Food Department
Checkerboard Square
St. Louis, Missouri 63164

Dear sir or madam,

Is it true that Ralston Purina has recently launched a new brand
of dog food called "Squirrel Blend"? The rumors circulating here
are that it even comes in two flavors: Woodland and Rocky
Mountain (chunky).

Personally I find this shocking, and so do almost all of my
colleagues working here at the Chicago office of TAC (The
Acronym Council). Can you please explain why feeding the
canines of America should warrant the systematic decimation
of the continent's peace-loving squirrel population? The dogs
are spoiled enough already.

Sincerely yours,

W. Stuart Wade

Ralston Purina Company

Grocery Products Group
Office of Consumer Affairs

August 5, 1992

Mr. W. Stuart Wade
3023 N. Clark St., Box 789
Chicago, IL 60657

Dear Mr. Wade:

Thank you for contacting us concerning Purina dog food products.

Ralston Purina Company does not manufacture a dog food product called
"Squirrel Blend" and I know of no plans to do so. I hope this
information will be helpful to you.

Again, thank you for your interest in Ralston Purina Company.

Sincerely,

Eileen Nixon

Eileen Nixon
Consumer Representative

Checkerboard Square
St. Louis, Missouri 63164

FNF 30561A-89A12

16

JAMES C. WADE III

P.O. Box 103
Montchoisi
1000 Lausanne 19
Switzerland

February 16th, 1995

State Farm Insurance Co.
Attn. Casualty Division - Statistics
One State Farm Plaza
Bloomington, Illinois 61701, USA

Dear sirs:

I've noticed that when a natural disaster hits, like an earthquake or hurricane, you can usually read in the paper within a few days that the insurance industry has estimated the total value of all the damage.

Do you also compile estimates on property damage from other causes? I work for a parents' rights organization called "Pro-Spank International" (in Singapore we're known as "Friends of the Cane"), and I would like to know if you could please furnish me with the latest available figures showing the $ value of the extensive damage caused each year by *children*. In my own household alone, it is quite a lot, so I can imagine that from a worldwide point of view, the total amount must be absolutely staggering.

If you have these data, could you please show a breakdown of the damage into the following categories:

1. Needlessly broken stereos, VCR's, expensive cameras, etc.

2. Scratched furniture, smashed antiques, broken heirlooms, etc.

3. Irretrievable loss of jewelry or other valuables (e.g. flushed down toilet)

4. Structural damage to dwelling unit

5. Stains

Any information you can provide along these lines will be extremely helpful to our cause. For example, I would like to use the statistics in a Pro-Spank P.R. brochure I am writing called *Those Damn Kids*.

Many thanks in advance for your kind assistance.

Yours sincerely,

[signature]

K. STEVE WILLIAMS, CPCU, CLU
VICE PRESIDENT-CLAIMS
PHONE (309) 766-2234

March 3, 1995

Mr. James C. Wade III
P. O. Box 103
Montchoisi
1000 Lausanne 19
Switzerland

Dear Mr. Wade:

I am responding to your request for information regarding property damage caused by children. We do not maintain specific loss data that would identify damage that might have resulted from the activities of children.

Sincerely,

K. Steve Williams
Vice President - Claims

KSW/LLS

JAMES C. WADE III

P.O. Box 103
Montchoisi
1000 Lausanne 19
Switzerland

September 4th, 1992

Learjet Corporation
Sales Department
8220 West Harry Street
Wichita, Kansas 67277
USA

Dear sirs,

I am writing on behalf of a client whom I represent, who has expressed an interest in purchasing two private jets for his and his wife's personal use.

After reviewing the product literature of your company, as well as that of your competitors, we are hoping now to narrow our search for the jets which best fit their needs. Could you please help us in this process by providing us with some additional information?

1. What is the maximum taxiing speed of your fastest model?

2. Would a Learjet be permitted to be used as a road vehicle in most countries? I think you would agree that a big cost saving could be incurred if my clients used their planes as luxury automobiles, too.

3. Your literature makes no specific mention of the presence on board of any spare tires or jack. Are these supplied? Should the need arise, would fixing a flat be difficult for a woman of medium build?

I would sincerely appreciate your responding to these questions so that my client and his wife can review Learjet's potential to meet their various transportation requirements.

Please reply <u>confidentially</u> to the above address, marking your letter in bold capital letters with the reference "Ming Zahoot." Thank you in advance for your cooperation.

Sincerely yours,

Learjet

Mr. **James C. WADE III**
P.O. Box 103
Montchoisi
1000 **Lausanne** 19

Geneva, September 30th, 1992

Re: **MING ZAHOOT**

Dear Sir,

Your letter dated September 4th, 1992, to **Learjet Corporation Sales Department**, in Wichita, has been forwarded to our Geneva office.

The undersigned, in charge of marketing and sales for **Learjet** Products in Europe and Africa, is delighted to provide you with answers to your questions.

1. The American Federal Aviation Administration approved flight manual stipulates that our airplane can be taxied with the assistance of the built in nose wheel steering at speeds up to 45 knots (83 km/h). Beyond this speed, the rudder is used to control the aircraft on the ground up to take off speed (135 knots/ 250 km/h).

2. I am afraid that we have no answer to this question.

3. We supply spare wheel(s) and tyre(s) as optional equipment.

We would be extremely pleased to speak with you at your earliest convenience.

In the meantime, we remain,

Yours sincerely,

Alain Ledoux
Regional Manager
Europe/ Africa

Encl. ment.

Suite 100, 5 Route de Chene • Ch-1207 Geneva, Switzerland • 41/22-786-1567 • Fax: 41/22-736-6179 • Telex: 428-388 KBS CH
Learjet Inc. a subsidiary of Bombardier Inc.

20

W. STUART WADE

3023 North Clark Street
Box 789
Chicago, Illinois 60657

August 28th, 1992

LaSalle National Bank
Attn. New Business Lending
120 S. LaSalle St.
Chicago, Illinois 60603

Dear sirs,

I am writing to you following the recent article in the magazine *Underdog Finance* in which your bank's policy toward start-up ventures was described. James Wade, my brother and business partner, and I were both very impressed with your generosity regarding no-interest loans and your overall willingness to try on new ideas. As the article suggested, I am coming to you today with a straightforward proposal costing less than $3 million.

Our concept is very simple, is not threatened by undue competition, and is based entirely on market research conducted by the independent firm of Creet Smooley & Busterbim. Their study showed that 61% of all 11-15 year-olds in the northern Chicago suburbs reported having "positive" or "very positive" attitudes toward tattoos. Out of this 61%, almost 90% said that the only reason they have not been tattooed themselves is that they do not know where to go to get one. Our business idea is to fulfill this unsatisfied demand by bringing the tattoos to the kids.

By leasing 100 Chevy vans, our strategy is to operate a fleet of mobile tattoo parlors which would cruise through affluent suburban neighborhoods (Evanston and further north) on weekends and after school, enabling young adults to be tattooed, under paramedical supervision, without travelling any further than the curb in front of their house.

Our project has just won the endorsement of the music group AC/DC, who have magnanimously allowed us to broadcast their music on the vans' 500-watt speakers, as a kind of attention-getter while the vans slowly drive through the target areas.

James and I would be happy to come see you and present our detailed business plan with five-year cash flow projections. I look forward to hearing from you regarding a convenient date for an appointment.

Sincerely,

W. Stuart Wade

Poste restante
Montchoisi Post Office
1000 Lausanne 19, Switzerland

September 22nd, 1992

LaSalle National Bank
New Lending Department
120 South LaSalle Street
Chicago, Illinois 60603 USA

Re: New venture, Mobile tattoo parlors

Dear sirs,

My brother and business partner Stuart Wade wrote to you last month describing our concept for a new business to meet the growing tattoo needs of affluent youngsters in the Near North suburbs. I thought I would write to give you a progress report.

I have been spending some time here in Europe discussing this venture with various banks, who have all been impressed with its scope and entrepreneurial daring. The president of one Swiss bank told me just this morning that it was the most interesting new venture he had seen since a group of investors sought his help in launching a special-interest magazine for Swiss Army Knife owners.

Five banks here have expressed an interest in joint financing through a kind of loan consortium. The total they would put up is $1.8 million, which leaves $1 million for another interested lender. As in all such cases, they would prefer that the financing would be anchored by a local bank, and I told them that we were dealing with LaSalle. This met with enthusiastic approval across the board.

Meanwhile, Stuart and I have negotiated a deal with a Korean firm for 100 "Kwik-Draw" tattooing machines to be installed in the vans. The "Kwik-Draw" is the most automated tattoo apparatus on the market, with precision needles and sophisticated high-speed robotics that function just like the pre-programmed arms that spot-weld doors on Hyundais. This gives us two big advantages. First, we can now handle up to 40 customers per van per school day (only 3 minutes per tattoo required, once we get the hang of the machinery). Second, since over 2,000 tattoo designs can be stored on a single diskette, we don't need to hire costly tattoo artists. This reduces our overall costs by 27%. We are negotiating further reductions with a German supplier of high-quality sub-dermal inks now.

May we have an appointment to see you and discuss the loan? I will be returning to Chicago in about three weeks. In the meantime I can be reached at the above address. I look forward to meeting you to talk about this exciting deal.

Sincerely,

22

120 South LaSalle Street
Chicago, Illinois 60603
(312) 781-8241

Lamont Change
Vice President

October 6, 1992

James C. Wade III
Poste restante
Montchoisi Post Office
1000 Lausanne 19, Switzerland

Dear Mr. Wade:

I am in receipt of your letter dated September 22, 1992. I
appreciate the opportunity to review your request. However, we do
not have a venture Capital Department. LaSalle is not interested
in participating in the bank group financing that you described.

Thank you for considering LaSalle National Bank.

Sincerely,

LC/ba

23

JAMES C. WADE III

P.O. Box 103
Montchoisi
1000 Lausanne 19
Switzerland

June 9th, 1994

Swiss Cheese Union AG
Attn. Marketing Director
Monbijoustrasse 45
3001 Bern

Dear sirs,

As you surely know, Americans are very health-conscious,
especially concerning the things they eat. For example,
Americans consume vast quantities of so-called "non-dairy"
coffee creams - an astonishing 175 kg per capita each year.
This fact prompted a brilliant idea that I would like to develop
with you as a Swiss export product for the U.S. market:
cheeseless fondue.

Could you please let me know if one of the cheesemaking regions
in Switzerland would be prepared to switch over production to a
100% non-dairy cheese? At this stage of my research, I am not
sure exactly what technology would be involved, perhaPS.merely a
simple extrusion process. We can discuss this later.

For now, if you would agree to work on the development of a
pre-packaged, all-biodegradable no-cheese fondue, I am convinced
that it would find great success in the USA. As an American,
and a lover of all things artificial, I would be an enthusiastic
partner in helping you realize the enormous potential of this
project. I look forward to your answer.

Yours sincerely,

Schweizerische Käseunion AG
Union suisse du commerce de fromage SA
Unione svizzera per il commercio del formaggio SA
Swiss Cheese Union Inc.

Monbijoustrasse 45
Postfach 8225

3001 Bern **ab 1.7.94**
Telefon (031) 371 33 31 (031) 378 11 11
Telefax (031) 372 11 76 (031) 378 11 12
Telex 912 404 scu

Mr.
James C. Wade III
P.O. Box 103
Montchoisi

1000 Lausanne 19

Berne, 16th June 1994 Li/Et

Dear Sir,

Thank you very much for your letter of 9th June 1994.

We regret to inform you that we are not interested in your proposal.

Yours sincerely,

SWISS CHEESE UNION INC.

[signatures]

JAMES C. WADE III

P.O. Box 103
Montchoisi
1000 Lausanne 19

June 20th, 1994

Swiss Cheese Union Inc.
Attn. Mr. P.P.A. Liechti
Monbijoustrasse 45
3001 Bern

Re: Cheeseless Fondue

Dear Mr. Liechti,

I have received your letter dated June 16th (also signed by another person whose name I can't quite make out - could it be N. Dranscan?) Whoever it is, thank you both for writing me back.

Regarding the content of your letter, I don't think I understood you very clearly. Do you have no interest in non-dairy cheese fondue at all? Don't forget, there are 265,000,000 consumers over in America. If every one of them had just one cheeseless fondue per year, that would be 265,000,000 fondues, which is a heck of a lot!

Or are you saying that you have no interest in developing it *right now?* If it's just a question of money, please take heart, because we could find plenty of wealthy partners. A big ad in *Readers Digest* would produce dozens of rich investors.

With your permission, I will draft an ad for you and contact the publisher. Meanwhile, can you please draw up a budget so we know how much money we need to get off the ground? It won't be cheap, but that "Cheeseless Fondue, Made in Switzerland" label will be worth its weight in gold!

Look forward to hearing from you again soon,

All the best to you and Mr. Dranscan,

Yours,

[signature]

Schweizerische Käseunion AG
Union suisse du commerce de fromage SA
Unione svizzera per il commercio del formaggio SA
Swiss Cheese Union Inc.

Monbijoustrasse 45
Postfach 8225

3001 Bern

ab 1.7.94

Telefon (031) 371 33 31   (031) 378 11 11
Telefax (031) 372 11 76   (031) 378 11 12
Telex   912 404 scu

Mr.
James C. Wade III
P.O. Box 103
Montchoisi

1000 Lausanne 19

Berne, 21st June 1994 Li/Et

Dear Sir,

As we have no interest in non-dairy cheese fondue at all, you understood the meaning of
our letter dated June 16th very clearly.

Yours sincerely,

SWISS CHEESE UNION INC.

[signatures]

27

3023 N. Clark Street, No. 789
Chicago, Illinois 60657
USA

September 18th, 1992

The Mayor,
Dorking,
Surrey RH4 1SJ
England

Dear Mr Mayor,

I teach a course in geography to an adult education class at the
Discover© Urban Nighttime Chicago Education center (DUNCE)™.
This semester we are studying English place names and were taken
aback to discover a town near London called "Dorking".

Could you possibly enlighten us as to how Dorking came to be
named Dorking? One of my students wonders whether this is
a verb form, although if that is true, we were none too sure exactly
what the meaning of the verb "to dork" might be. Several
suggestions were put forward, none very nice.

We look forward to your comments.

Sincerely yours,

W. Stuart Wade

PS. If you are casting about for a sister city, may we suggest
   Gland, Switzerland?

MOLE VALLEY DISTRICT COUNCIL

Pippbrook,
Dorking, Surrey RH4 1SJ
Tel: Dorking (0306) 885001
FAX (0306) 876821

Chairman of the Council
Bill Lancaster

25th September, 1992

Dear Mr. Wade,

Thank you very much for your letter of the 18th September and your interest in the name of our town.

I have recently had cause to ask this question of Dr. Bird, the Principal Archeologist at Surrey County Council, on behalf of someone else so luckily I have his explanation readily available for you!

"**The name of Dorking:** this is somewhat enigmatic, because it seems that no-one can satisfactorily explain the first element. The second element is -ingas, which means something like 'followers of' or 'dwellers at', and is related to the German word which gives -ingen at the end of many names of south German towns. The first element has been variously explained as the old name of the River Mole or an old English personal name 'Deorc', hence 'people living by the Dorce' or 'the people of Deorc', but there seems to be no independent support for the river or personal name"

The enigma continues. From holidays spent in the States I have become aware that the term 'dork' is probably not flattering. I do not think that the term has anything to do with our town. I think I see the meaning behind your letter!

I am also enclosing a copy of the official guide to the District which I hope may be of interest to you.

Yours sincerely,

Chairman of the Council

Mr. W. S. Wade,
3023 North Clark Street #789,
Chicago,
IL 60657,
U.S.A.

29

JAMES C. WADE III

P.O. Box 103
Montchoisi
1000 Lausanne 19
Switzerland

June 29th, 1992

The School of Paralegal Studies
2245 Perimeter Park
Atlanta, Georgia 30341
USA

Dear sirs,

I am very interested in enrolling in your school.

I have been fascinated by paralegal phenomena since I was a small
child. My first encounter with the paralegal was at the age of seven,
when our cat suddenly walked up a wall of our living room, turned
upside down and ran across the ceiling barking like a dog. Later,
when I was in college, I wrote a paper in Religious Studies on Satan's
probable return to Earth in the guise of a talk show host. I got an A.
My favorite movie of all time is "The Omen, Part 3".

The reason I mention these things is to show how serious my
commitment to the supernatural and unexplainable really is.

Until I saw the ad for your school, I had no idea that a place for
non-scientists existed that was devoted to studying the paralegal and
other occult matters. I would definitely consider moving to Atlanta
and entering your school. Can you please tell me if you teach your
students how to communicate with the dead? How much is tuition?

Looking forward to hearing from you, I am

Yours sincerely,

[signature]

PS. Why does the name "Perimeter Park" seem so familiar?
Is that where they discovered that gruesome cannibalistic
ritual a few years back?

JAMES C. WADE III

P.O. Box 103
Montchoisi
1000 Lausanne 19
Switzerland

September 4th, 1992

The School of Paralegal Studies
2245 Perimeter Park
Atlanta, Georgia 30341
USA

Dear sirs,

Last June 29th, I wrote to you about enrolling in your school to study the paralegal. I was hoping to enter in the fall term, but I did not hear anything from you during the entire summer, and I suppose it's too late for me now.

What gives? Aren't you interested in getting new students? Is it still possible for me to get in? If so, I would sure appreciate your letting me know.

Yours,

[signature]

PS. Is there a reading list for the autumn semester? I have already read the *Necronomicon* and the *Egyptian Book of the Dead*, but I'm sure there must be other books I should get. Please let me know so I can order them and not lose any time. Thank you.

PROFESSIONAL CAREER DEVELOPMENT INSTITUTE

6065 Roswell Road • Suite 3118 • Atlanta, Georgia 30328 • 404-451-2300 or 800-223-4542

James C. Wade III
P.O. Box 103
Montchoisi
1000 Lausanne 19 Switzerland

Dear Mr. Wade:

I am writing in response to the letters which you have written to us in recent months regarding your interest in our programs.

I think you may be confused about what it is that we do here at The School of Paralegal Studies. I believe you have mistaken the word "paralegal" for the word "paranormal." Paralegal is a general term used to describe a person who assists an attorney in the practice of the law. The term paranormal is used to describe phenomena outside accepted usual (or "normal") physical possibility, as well as the occult. Certainly, some of the experiences you have described are within the realm of the paranormal; your cat's behavior, for example, is rather unusual.

I believe that your interest in studies of unusual and paranormal phenomena is a genuine one. While I do not know of any, I do not doubt that there are many fine programs of that type, and I wish you the best of luck in finding one that suits your needs.

Finally, let me mention to you that one of the books you refer to, <u>The Necronomicon</u>, is a purely fictional work by the American fantasy writer H.P. Lovecraft, who wrote it as a literary exercise.

Karl Freedman
Chief Instructor
The School of Paralegal Studies

W. STUART WADE

3023 North Clark St., No. 789
Chicago, Illinois 60657

July 7th, 1992

Cleveland Indians Baseball Team
Attn. Staff Psychologist
Cleveland Stadium
Cleveland, Ohio 44114

Dear sir or madam,

Pursuant to a research grant given to me by the National Institute of Mental Health (NIMH), I am preparing a study entitled *Hypothalamic Post-Influences on Cognitive Processes and Non-Random Determinism among Professional Baseball Players.* I would like to request the assistance of the Indians, my favorite team.

What I propose is that the team members be fitted with electrodes during the course of a game or two. The electrodes will monitor pre-frontal lobe activity in the brain as well as reptilian brainstem function. The data collected will be fed into a computer to try to arrive at a predictive model of operant infield vs. outfield behavior, neo-Skinnerian pitcher-batter conflicts, and the so-called "third baseman syndrome", which as you know almost always leads to problems.

In case you are concerned about the possible detrimental effect on the public image of the team, let me say you have nothing to worry about. Since the players all wear caps, the electrodes would be invisible to people in the stands or television viewers. Only a close-up shot might reveal a few loose wires here and there, but I'm sure that can be explained away.

On the other hand, you could publicly announce your support for the research, which might even garner some P.R. brownie points for you. (It could also help me secure my next grant, to study eating disorders among the U.S. Congress.)

May I trouble you to confirm your participation, so that I can begin arranging for the various brain equipment? Many thanks in advance for your reply.

Yours sincerely,

W. Stuart Wade

Cleveland Indians   *Cleveland Stadium   Cleveland, Ohio 44114   (216) 861-1200   Fax 566-1287*

5 August 92

Dear Mr. Wade:

I am in receipt of your note of July 7th regarding a proposal
to enlist the help of a number of Indian ballplayers in an
experiment for your research purposes.

Unfortunately, while the Indians organization would like to
accomodate as many requests as possible, especially those
from a scientific research team, I'm afraid that your request
won't be able to be honored by the team.

I'm sorry about this development, because it is clear that
you have done a great deal of preparation in this field. However,
I do wish you the best of luck in finding another organization
that can better accomodate your needs at this time.

Thanks for your understanding, and all best wishes.

Sincerely,

Rick Wolff
Roving Psychological Coach

34

JAMES C. WADE III

P.O. Box 103
Montchoisi
1000 Lausanne 19
Switzerland

March 26th, 1992

Euro Disney
Attn. the Personnel Manager
P. O. Box 103
F-77777 Marne-La-Vallée Cedex 4
France

<u>Job Application</u>

Dear sir,

I am extremely excited about the imminent opening of a Disneyland here in Europe, and I am writing to enquire whether I might be able to secure employment at Euro Disney. What I would like, in fact, is to play the role of Mickey Mouse himself. Although I have not had any directly related career positions up to now, I feel I would do a good job.

In addition, I have some skills which I think could make Euro Mickey a much more innovative, more interesting Mouse than the one we all know and love back in the USA. For example, with the help of tiny suction cups, I could climb vertical surfaces for a very crowd-pleasing effect. Imagine the excitement if the European Mickey Mouse were a kind of human fly! Not only would I greet the kids, but I could also scale the walls of Main Street USA, maybe even spreading batlike wings and swooping down on the crowd below. Imagine the happiness in the beaming faces of all those children!

Please let me know if this might interest you. I could come to France for an audition without delay. Looking forward to hearing from you soon, I am

Yours sincerely,

[signature]

PS. Note for for Wardrobe Department: I wear a size
      40 regular suit.

Casting

Mr. James WADE III
P.O. BOX 103
Montchoisi
CH 1000 LAUSANNE 19
SUISSE

Noisy le Grand,
May 26th, 1992

Dear Mr. WADE III,

Thank you for your recent letter expressing an interest in Euro Disney Resort.

To help us better evaluate your background and qualifications, could you please send us your curriculum vitae (English/French) with the reference : BIO/249952.

We look forward to hearing from you soon and truly appreciate your interest in our Company.

Sincerely,

Anne VINCENT
Employment Representative

Euro Disney S.C.A.
Gérant : Euro Disney S.A.

BOITE POSTALE 110
F-77777 MARNE LA VALLEE C

33 (1) 49 32 49 32 Tél
33 (1) 49 32 46 46 Fax

Société en Commandite par actions au capital de 1.700.000.000 F   RCS Meaux B 334 173 887

JAMES C. WADE III

P.O. Box 103
Montchoisi
1000 Lausanne 19
Switzerland

June 26th, 1992

Euro Disney
Attn. Ms. Anne Vincent,
Employment Representative, Casting
P. O. Box 110
F-77777 Marne-La-Vallée Cedex 4
France

Ref. BIO/249952

Dear Ms. Vincent,

Thank you very much for your letter to me of May 26th. I was glad
to hear from you. I have spent some time putting together my
resumé, which is enclosed.

Unfortunately I am not able to send you a French version just yet, as
I still need a bit of time to get my French up to the level where I can
use it to exaggerate my job qualifications, as is the English custom.
However, I am sure that my spoken French would be more than
sufficient for 99% of Euro-Mickey's on-the-job requirements
(example: "Bonjour, kids!" + friendly wave).

I look forward to hearing from you again soon, and thank you
once again for considering me in the role of Mickey "the Human
Fly" Mouse.

Yours sincerely,

James Wade

RESUME of James C. Wade III

Birthdate:	March 9th, 1957
Place of birth:	New Smolensk, Indiana, USA
Citizenship:	American

Education:

1962-1968	Beltz G. Milderson Elementary School, New Smolensk, Ind. (crossing guard, Arithmetic Club, Show and Tell Society)
1968-1971	Melville Cray Junior High School, New Smolensk, Ind. (double major in gym and shop. Squad leader, annual "Basketball with the Elderly" tournament)
1971-1974	Pigeon Creek Rural Consolidated High School, New Smolensk, Ind. (Treasurer, Useless Histrionics Club, four-year Letterman on Varsity Fishing Team, Pep Club, intramural shotgun marksmanship)
1974-1978	Massachusetts Institute of Technology, Cambridge, Mass. (double major in particle physics and German. Thesis subject: "Use of the word 'das' in the Uncertainty Principle of Werner Karl Heisenberg." Member of Alpha Beta Gamma Delta Etc. fraternity. Organized annual Nobel Laureate Singalong.)
1978-1982	Max Planck Institute, Untersindelfingerheimen schwanden, W. Germany. Post-graduate work in shoe design. Member of inter-disciplinary team studying effects of charcoal filters in cordovan wingtips.

Employment:

1982-1987	Bud's Mouth Organs, Chicago, Illinois. Worked first two years as salesman. Exceeded sales targets. Met Neil Young. Last three years as head of repair unit, where I increased throughput by 26%.
1987-	Ace Veterinarian Supply, Lausanne, Switzerland. Turtle and horse specialist. Voted Man of the Year '92 by Swiss Rinderpest Society.

Special Skills and Interests:

Tennis, skiing, travel, clandestine photography, travel, farm implements. Experienced in hand-to-hand combat, macramé. Fluent in Korean. Health excellent, slight limp.

References:

Mr. Rollo Greb, Manager, Bud's Mouth Organs, Chicago; Rev. William Tecumseh Buttwig, Elm Street Grill, New Smolensk; Mr. A.T.C. Grimbo, Holy Roller Moving and Storage, New Smolensk

JAMES C. WADE III

P.O. Box 103
Montchoisi
CH - 1000 Lausanne 19
Switzerland

August 3rd, 1992

Euro Disney
Attn. Ms. Anne Vincent,
Employment Representative, Casting
P. O. Box 110
F-77777 Marne-La-Vallée Cedex 4
France

Ref: BIO/249952, M. Mouse, extra skills

Dear Ms. Vincent,

At the end of June I sent you my resumé, as per your request. I hope you received it and have had a chance to look it over. You will find my background a good fit with your requirements, and I look forward to hearing from you in due course.

In the meantime, I have been working on a kind of "utility belt" for Euro-Mickey, which will contain various tools I think he might need in order to fulfill the special role I have in mind for him. I am trying to keep these tools limited to the absolute necessities, mainly for reasons of weight. So far, I have him outfitted with a length of nylon rope, carabiners, pitons, a grappling hook, a small block-and-tackle device, a flare gun, and some super glue. Eventually I may add some kind of parachute, possibly also an inflatable life vest.

One question has cropped up which I hope you can answer: Does Mickey have opposable thumbs? I never really noticed before, but I need to know for the design of certain features, such as a lightweight crowd control prod, etc.

I am certainly excited about the prospect of taking on this historic role, and await the green light from you!

Yours sincerely,

JAMES C. WADE III

P.O. Box 103
Montchoisi
1000 Lausanne 19
Switzerland

November 9th, 1992

Logitech Switzerland
European Headquarters
111 Romanel-sur-Morges
Switzerland

Attn. <u>Mouse Department</u>

Dear sirs,

Over the past several months, I have been involved in some very
delicate negotiations with the people at Euro Disney regarding my
employment in their theme park outside Paris. In fact, I am well on
the way to claiming the prized role of Mickey Mouse himself. My
qualifications (if I may be immodest) are exceptionally well-matched
to the challenging requirements of this position. At church bingo
the other day I met one of your directors, Dr. Geronimo Anderson,
who told me that Logitech also has something to do with mice. I
didn't exactly follow his train of thought, as he kept drifting off into
some technical lingo. At any rate, I gather from his comments that
your company has put together some kind of specialized mouse
know-how, so I was wondering if you could help me prepare for my
Disney audition, which will undoubtedly be coming up soon.

Could Logitech provide me with any literature (better yet, tutorial
sessions) on any of the following activities: squeaking, sniffing
the air, scurrying for cover, frightening housewives, frightening
elephants (are the same techniques used?), greeting foreign digni-
taries, product endorsement, and first aid?

Many thanks in advance.

Yours sincerely,

[signature]

PS. Dr Anderson gave me the number of your mouse hotline, but
frankly they were no help at all.

Logitech Suisse
1122 Romanel-sur-Morges
Switzerland

James C. Wade III
BP 103 Montchoisi
1000 Lausanne 19

Romanel / Morges, November 16th, 1992

Dear Mr. Wade,

I have received your letter asking for help and tution on mouse matters. I am very pleased to hear that you are being selected for such an important role. As the leading manufacturer of computer mice, our main level of expertice lies in the technological aspects of the rodental topic, hence the technical lingo Dr. Anderson was using. I am sorry to hear that our mouse hotline was useless, but as they are only reponsible for technical matters, I am not surprised that they could not help you.

As a matter of policy, Logitech does not give tuition on how to be an sucessful mouse, as we feel it is a bit like giving our competitive advantage away. However, Mickey is the most revered beacon of the mouse community and the perfect case study of the sucessful mouse, so the upkeep of its image is something we feel very stongly about. The character of Mickey Mouse is owned by the Walt Disney Corp. but it's also Logitech's duty to ensure Mickey is portrayed at its best.

After discussing the matter with our top managers, I propose we meet for lunch and discuss a coaching programme we should organise. You can reach me at the following number: 021.869.98.60.
Unfortunately, our expertise in housewife/elephant scaring is limited, so I don't think you should rely solely on Logitech for your mouse training.

Awaiting your phone call, I remain,

Yours sincerely,

Ludovic Patry
Logitech SA

PS: By the way, Dr. Anderson's fist name is not Geronimo, but Ramses.

Casting

• • •

Mr. James C. WADE
P.O. Box 103
Montchoisi
CH-1000 LAUSANNE 19
SUISSE

Noisy le Grand,
December 28th, 1992

Dear Mr. WADE,

We have received your recent letter expressing an interest in employment
opportunities with Euro Disney Resort.

We have reviewed your background and qualifications with regard to our
employment needs and are unable to offer you a position which would
correspond to your profile.

We are sorry we cannot be more encouraging. We do, however, appreciate
your interest in our Company and wish you success in your future endeavours.

Sincerely,

Karin BOVIN
Employment Representative

Euro Disney S.C.A.
Gérant : Euro Disney S.A.

BOITE POSTALE 110
F-77777 MARNE LA VALLEE CEDEX 4

33 (1) 49 32 49 32 Tél
33 (1) 49 32 46 46 Fax

Société en Commandite par actions au capital de 1.700.000.000 F   RCS Meaux B 334 173 887

42

JAMES C. WADE III

P.O. Box 103
Montchoisi
1000 Lausanne 19
Switzerland

January 11th, 1993

Egon Zehnder Associates,
International Executive Search
Attn. Mr. Egon Zehnder himself
Toblerstrasse 80
8044 Zurich, Switzerland

Dear Egon,

I have just returned from an upbeat Christmas vacation to find that
Euro Disney, after dithering for months, has decided not to hire me
to play the part of Mickey Mouse at their theme park. My qualifications were excellent, but, as ludicrous as this sounds, they found
someone else more to their liking.

Needless to say, I am crushed.

Now I must pick up the pieces of my shattered life and go on, hard
as that may be. You have some experience with job placement, don't
you? Maybe you have some ideas where I could go from here. Do
you think you would be able to find me an appropriate opening
somewhere? As you can see from my resumé (copy enclosed), I am
certainly suited to a top management position, maybe a board-level
thing somewhere. Failing that, please note my interests in swimming and horseback riding.

Looking forward to a positive response from you, I am

Sincerely yours,

James Wade

Mr. James C. Wade III
P.O. Box 103, Montchoisi
1000 Lausanne 19

January 14, 1993

Dear Jim,

Thank you for your letter of January 11th with your curriculum vitae and Euro Disney correspondence attached. I can well understand why you're crushed: it's unbelievable in what sloppy way a company like Disney could handle a situation that is obviously very important to you. Could it be that Euro Disney belongs to those companies that have been awarded with one of your hilarious letters? And what would have made them even more angry, that the correspondence wasn't published in your great book "P.S. My Bush Pig's Name is Boris"?

As you know doubt understand, I would like to be helpful to you in your job search. Unfortunately, Egon Zehnder International as management consultants work only for client companies in advising them on the appointment of their very senior executives to fill key positions in their organizations. Our ability to be of help to you therefore depends on our firm working on a mandate calling for someone of your background, qualifications, experience and unique talents.

We are at the moment carrying out a careful review of our current assignments and you may rest assured that we will be in touch with you as soon as we see a client situation that might be of apparent mutual interest. In the meantime, the alternative of swimming and horseback riding doesn't look that bad either. Does it?

Keep me posted on your decisions and, in the meantime consider the investment of Sfr. 20.-- to join the Harvard Club of Switzerland!!!

With best personal regards,

Egon P.S. Zehnder

W. STUART WADE

3023 N. Clark Street, No. 789
Chicago, Illinois 60657

October 26th, 1992

Hormel & Co.
Mr. Richard M. Knowlton,
Chief Executive Officer
501 16th Avenue NE
Austin, Minnesota 55912

Dear Mr. Knowlton,

The Persian Gulf is a part of the world we have all become more familiar with in recent times, wouldn't you agree?

I couldn't help but wonder why the straits at the mouth of the Gulf share the same name as your company, Hormel. Were you founded in the Middle East, or were the Straits of Hormel actually named for the Hormel family? If so, I can imagine they must have done something pretty remarkable to get a geographic feature like that named after them. Or was it just that the Arabs and Iranians living there like canned beans and chili?

U.S. corporate history is a hobby of mine. In the last few years I have even written an article here and there on some of the more interesting episodes in the lives of some of our better-known corporations and their products. For example, I wrote a longish piece on the Allies' extensive use of Ben-Gay in WWII for the magazine *Balms, Ointments & Salves*, and on the history of the Barcalounger for *Chair News*. I'm currently working on a lavish coffee-table book describing the role of Shake'n'Bake in contemporary society.

I am certain there's a fascinating story behind this Straits business and I'd love to hear it if you have the time.

Yours sincerely,

W. Stuart Wade

Geo. A. Hormel & Company
P.O. Box 800 / Austin, Minnesota 55912

Executive Offices
R. L. Knowlton
Chairman and Chief Executive Officer
Tel: (507) 437-5357
Fax: (507) 437-5489

January 8, 1993

Mr. W. Stuart Wade
3023 North Clark St. #789
Chicago, IL   60657

Dear Mr. Wade:

Thanks so much for your letter concerning the
Persian Gulf. I have learned through our people
that the area you probably are referring to is
called the Strait of Hormuz. It is not the Strait
of Hormel. The spelling undoubtedly caused the
confusion.

I wish we had a more dramatic answer for you, but
I am pleased to tell you that the name Hormel is
becoming more and more a household word around the
world.

Thanks so much for thinking of us.

Sincerely,

R. L. KNOWLTON

kj

46

JAMES C. WADE III

P.O. Box 103, Montchoisi
1000 Lausanne 19
Switzerland

October 30th, 1993

Carter-Wallace Inc.
Attn. Condom Dept.
1345 Avenue of the Americas
New York, New York 10105
USA

Dear sirs,

I remember reading in *Scientific American* that a company in the States has just introduced a new brand of musical condoms. I'm not sure how they work — some kind of hydraulic system, I think — but evidently they play a melody when "in use". Are you the manufacturer, by any chance?

If so, I would be very grateful if you could pass on an order of mine to one of your distributors in the Chicago area. I would like to have some delivered to my brother who lives there.

Could you please arrange to send two dozen musical condoms to the following address: Father Stuart Wade, c/o St. Maude's, 3023 N. Clark Street, Box 789, Chicago, Illinois 60657. Please have them bill me at my address above, or else let me know how I should pay you.

My order:

Tune	Size	Quantity
Ravel's Bolero	L	6
Stars and Stripes Forever	L	6
Colonel Bogey's March	L	3
Can't Get No Satisfaction	M	3
TOTAL		18

I would appreciate it if you could confirm to me whether you can fill this order. It is very important that Stuart receives them in time for Christmas. Many thanks in advance,

Yours sincerely,

[signature]

47

2 RESEARCH WAY, PRINCETON, NEW JERSEY 08540-6628, U.S.A.

INTERNATIONAL
DIVISION

November 18, 1993

James C. Wade III
P O Box 103, Montchoisi
1000 Lausanne 19
Switzerland

Dear Mr. Wade:

This acknowledges receipt of your October 30th request for two dozen musical condoms.

Kindly be informed that Carter-Wallace, Inc., manufacturer of Trojan, Mentor, Magnum and Class Act Brand condoms, does not manufacture musical condoms; thus, we are unable to fill your order.

Sincerely,

Barbara Schechter
Director of Marketing

BS/lw

W. STUART WADE

3023 N. Clark Street, No. 789
Chicago, Illinois 60657
USA

August 12th, 1992

Mr. Sherlock Holmes
221b Baker Street
London
England

Dear Mr. Holmes,

Circumstances surrounding the demise of my acquaintance Festus
Maytag lead me to believe he was brutally murdered. However
the police have already closed the case, saying it was a suicide.

True, Festus's stomach was full of Prestone antifreeze and sleeping
pills, he was found hanged with a note in his unique handwriting
thoughtfully pinned to his shirt, consisting of the single word:
"suicide." Even so, this macabre scene has the unmistakable whiff
of fraud about it. I simply can think of no reason why Festus would
take his own life, other than the ugly divorce he was facing and the
abysmal failure of his business, Cartons USA.

What steps would you suggest I take to investigate this incident on
my own? I have very little money to spend on a private investigator.
If only I had your prowess in this field....

Respectfully yours,

W. Stuart Wade

PS. Could it have been an accident?

Mr. W. Stuart Wade
3023 North Clark Street #789
Chicago, IL 60657
USA

Dear Mr. Stuart Wade,

Mr Holmes thanks you for your recent letter and has asked
me to reply on his behalf.

As you may be aware, Mr Holmes has now retired to Sussex
where he spends his time reviewing the records of his
cases and keeping bees.

In his own words, Mr Holmes has given himself up entirely
"to that soothing life of nature for which I had so often
yearned during the long years amid the gloom of London."

He is nevertheless, delighted to be the recipient of your
letter and sends you his cordial regards.

Yours sincerely

Erica Harper

Erica Harper
. Secretary to Sherlock Holmes

P.S. If Mr. Holmes was still investigating I am sure he
would find your case very interesting.

**The Secretary to Sherlock Holmes,
Abbey National plc, 221b Baker Street, London.**

W. STUART WADE

3023 N. Clark Street, No. 789
Chicago, Illinois 60657
USA

October 16th, 1993

Victorinox Cutlery Co.
Attn. Swiss Army Knife Dept.
6438 Ibach-Schwyz
Switzerland

Dear sirs,

Do you make a Swiss Army Switchblade? I am a high school
student here in Chicago and my numerous associates and I could
foresee placing a large order.

Thank you in advance for your reply.

Sincerely yours,

W. Stuart Wade

PS. There would be no need for a corkscrew, as we are all under
the legal drinking age.

VICTORINOX CH-6438 Ibach-Schwyz

Telephon: 043/23 13 43
Telex: 866 073 vis ch
Telefax: 043/21 73 21
Bahnstation: Schwyz
Postcheckkonto: 60-94-0

Sparkasse, Schwyz
Kantonalbank, Schwyz
Schweiz. Kreditanstalt SZ
Schweiz. Bankverein Schwyz
Schweiz. Bankgesellschaft SZ

W. Stuart Wade
3023 North Clark Street 789
Chicago, IL 60657
USA

U/Ref. EX/la   6438 Ibach, 19.10.93

Dear Mr. Wade

Thank you for your letter of October 16.

Please be informed that we do not manufacture Swiss Army Switch
blades since it is forbidden in Switzerland to sell Switch blade
knives.

Yours sincerely,

V I C T O R I N O X

52

JAMES C. WADE III

P.O. Box 103
Montchoisi
CH - 1000 Lausanne 19
Switzerland

April 12th, 1992

American Kite Flier's Association
1559 Rockville Pike
Rockville MD 20852
USA

Dear sirs,

I learned of the existence of your organization after watching the exploits of your secretary-general Mr Perez-de Cuellar on a recent BBC documentary. May I congratulate you on being able to attract him to your association after his retirement from the UN.

Although I would not consider myself an expert kite flier, I have had some success in designing kites made out of unusual materials. I am presently having some difficulties with a rather large kite I am working on (it will be about nine feet by five) and wondered if anyone at your association has any experience with tubular steel and cowhide?

Looking forward to hearing from you soon,

Yours sincerely,

[signature]

AMERICAN KITEFLIERS ASSOCIATION
1559 Rockville Pike, Rockville, Maryland 20852 • Phone or Fax (408) 647-8483

Tuesday, June 16, 1992

James C. Wade III
PO Box 103, Montchoisi
CH-1000 Lausanne 19
Switzerland

Dear Mr. Wade III,

Thanks for your kind letter regarding the American Kitefliers Association.

I am chagrined to find that despite our best efforts towards protecting the privacy of our members that the media have again shown no sensitivity, and let the word out about Sr. Perez. I must admit, though, that enticing him into the ranks of AKA was easy—we simply offered cool breezes, which must have been a relief after all that hot air.

Although it's hard to tell from your description, the main problem with your kite may be that you are using the cowhide hair-to-windward. Try it the other way for less turbulence. Also, ensure that your steel is no heavier than .00046 chrome-moly 38-296 tubing, or you'll have no end of grief finding suitable cross-tees and end fittings.

I'd suggest either a six-point or ten-point bridle, depending on the plumbing of your cowhide, and strongly recommend that you orient it tail down.

As problems of the sort you are having don't come before us every day, I have taken the liberty of sharing them with our membership by publishing your letter in the July issue of our bi-monthly newsletter *Kiting*.

We would be honored if you were to see fit to join our ranks. We have few representatives in the high country, and can use a creative European correspondent.

Chin Up,

Brooks G. Leffler
Executive Director

54

JAMES C. WADE III

P.O. Box 103
Montchoisi
1000 Lausanne 19
Switzerland

September 7th, 1992

Lane Fox, Estate Agents
15 Half Moon Street
London W1Y 8AT
England

Dear sirs,

My family and I shall be relocating to England early next year in connection with my work for the Banque Finno-Ugrique (Suisse) S.A., which is setting up a private banking office in London.

As we are a large family (nine children under the age of eight), we would very much like to settle outside London if possible. I was given the name of your firm by Mr. Delaware Undertwig who thought you could help us find a suitable house in one of the Home Counties.

For reasons of family tradition, I would particularly like to find a house shaped like the letter "W". Mr. Undertwig thought this would not present a problem for your firm, as he himself bought a country home two years ago with your help which, if I understood him correctly, was built entirely out of hardened gum resin. Your specialty in locating such unusual accommodations is much appreciated, and that is why I have chosen to work with you.

In addition, I should also mention that the nature of my business requires a certain amount of precaution as to the safety of myself and my family. Therefore I would insist upon the house in question having some kind of electrified fence and moat system surrounding it. Furthermore it must be capable of withstanding a blast of at least five megatons of TNT.

Have you anything in mind for us? I look forward to hearing from you at the above postal address.

Many thanks,

Surveyors and Estate Agents
Commercial Property Consultants

Lane Fox

15 Half Moon Street
London W1Y 8AT
Fax 071-408 1308
071-499 4785

10th September 1992
HHH/DJL/HH2

James C Wade III
PO Box 103
Montchoisi
1000 Lausanne 19
Switzerland

Dear Mr Wade

We were interested to receive your letter dated 7th September and to
learn of your wish to purchase a Country House of unusual design,
structure and size to accommodate your large family.

We do not recall assisting with the purchase of a House constructed of
hardened gum resin although Cob Houses (a traditional West Country
building material of hardened dung and mud) do occasionally come to the
market. The shape you require may also present a problem as a 'W' is
seldom found although a 'K' 'J' 'O' 'E' may be easier.

We appreciate your requirement for security although we would hope that
a secluded country House, with or without a moat, where a high degree of
privacy could be achieved might be suitable for you. We would not be
able to specify prior to purchase whether a property was able to
withstand a blast of 5 megatons but we would be very glad to arrange for
blast testing to be carried out subsequent to your purchase so that this
aspect of security can be fully measured.

Should you wish us to proceed with a search on your behalf we would be
grateful if you could please complete the enclosed questionnaire which
will provide us with the necessary information we require in order to
locate a suitable home. Furthermore, when you are next in this country,
I would be interested to meet you and learn more of the structure of Mr
Undertwig's gum House.

Yours sincerely

H T HOLLAND-HIBBERT

56

JAMES C. WADE III

P.O. Box 103
Montchoisi
1000 Lausanne 19
Switzerland

September 22nd, 1992

Lane Fox, Estate Agents
Mr. H. T. Holland-Hibbert, Associate Director
15 Half Moon Street
London W1Y 8AT
England

Dear Mr. Holland-Hibbert,

Thank you for your letter of the 10th. I appreciate your candor with regard to the likelihood of meeting my conditions for a country estate.

Concerning the shape of the house: we Wades have lived in W-shaped houses since 1985, which perhaps stretches the word "tradition" a bit far, but is nevertheless something we take rather seriously. For your dossier, please note that houses shaped like "J" "O" "K" or "E" would be undesirable as would those shaped like "F" "U" or "N". We would however settle for an "M", in which case my family and I would simply reorient ourselves "hair-to-windward", as they say.

In either case, I cannot stress the security factor enough. Have you really not got any blast-test data on the houses you represent? This surprises me. The villa I own here in Switzerland was certified by the builder to be able to survive a direct hit by a tactical nuclear device. This has been a great comfort to my family. (Happily, my business dealings have not come to that.)

I have not filled out your questionnaire, as it makes no attempt whatsoever to identify my special needs. For example, nowhere on the form can I express my wish for armor plating in the TV room. That said, I trust you will keep me posted of any suitable properties that do come on the market. Price is not an object.

Yours sincerely,

[signature]

PS. I spoke again to Mr Undertwig about his house and he confirms it was 2/3 dung.

57

JAMES C. WADE III

P.O. Box 103
Montchoisi
1000 Lausanne 19
Switzerland

June 3rd, 1992

Executive Book Summaries, Inc.
5 Main Street
Bristol, Vermont 05443-1398
USA

Dear sirs,

I read your ad about 15-minute executive summaries of business books: *terrific idea!* How often - for mere lack of time and interest - have I had to pass up the chance to read some of the latest thinking on vital corporate issues such as competitive strategic excellence, total quality strategy, global strategic competition, or any other combination of these words. Do you also have non-business-oriented titles in your product range? If so, may I place the following order for books I simply have never found time to read properly? Thank you!

Please rush me an executive summary of:

+ Faust
+ Pride and Prejudice
+ The Brothers Karamazov
+ Moby Dick (I've already read Cliff's Notes, but found them vaguely unsatisfying)
+ Great American Short Stories
+ Websters Collegiate Dictionary
+ Rand McNally Atlas of the World

Again, many thanks for your wonderful service. I look forward to hearing from you soon.

Yours sincerely,

SOUNDVIEW Executive Book Summaries

5 Main Street, Bristol, Vermont 05443   (802) 453-4062

July 3, 1992

Mr. James C. Wade III
P.O. Box 103
Montchoisi
1000 Lausanne 10
Switzerland

Dear Mr. Wade:

   Thanks for your recent inquiry concerning Soundview book summaries.
   Unfortunately, we have not summarized any of the books on your list (Faust, Moby Dick, et al).
   However, we intend to tackle Websters Collegiate Dictionary right after completing one of our more difficult projects to date: an eight-page summary of The Encyclopaedia Britannica.
   We'll keep you posted on our progress; thanks again.

Warmly,

Jeff Olson
Editor

JAMES C. WADE III

P.O. Box 103
Montchoisi
1000 Lausanne 19
Switzerland

August 26th, 1992

Development Specialists, Inc.
Three First National Plaza
70 West Madison Street, Suite 2300
Chicago, Illinois 60602
USA

Dear sirs,

I am interested in discussing financing possibilities with you for a business venture to be based on a new invention of mine. It is my understanding that you will review solid business opportunities, providing seed capital up to the amount of $100 million. Good news: I will only need half that much.

My invention is a small, comfortable device which aids communication for the deaf and hearing-impaired. It is worn not by the deaf person himself but rather by the person with normal hearing who wishes to speak with a deaf person. The device fits over the mouth and converts the spoken words of the person wearing it into speech bubbles, like in an ordinary comic book. By looking just above the head of the user, deaf persons can read what people are saying to them. After about fifteen seconds, the speech bubbles simply dissolve.

I think you'll agree with me that the global market potential for such a product is enormous. I therefore foresee setting up production in a low-cost location, such as Bangladesh or Alabama, and building up a worldwide distribution network.

I am also working on a prototype which would produce thought bubbles, but am having difficulties with the "cloud" look which convention requires.

Assuming a positive outcome in *State of Wisconsin v. State of Minnesota*, I see no reason why this venture should not be successful. Would DSI be interested in getting in on the ground floor?

I look forward very much to your suggestions as to a next step.

Yours sincerely,

James Wade

60

**Development
Specialists, Inc.**

Management Consulting Services in the Areas of:
Reorganization · Bankruptcy · Turnaround Management · Business Workouts

23 September 1992

Mr. James C. Wade III
Post Office Box 103
Montchoisi
1000 Lausanne 19
Switzerland

    Re: <u>Communication Device for the Deaf</u>

Dear Mr. Wade:

Your letter to our offices of 26 August 1992 has been handed to
me for review and response. Needless to say, our firm is quite
intrigued by both the concept and the device you suggest might be
developable through your efforts.

However, before we can proceed to further evaluate the potential
of this proposition there are two items of information we would
require. Initially, and with respect to what I would suspect
would be the easier piece of information, our offices are quite
unaware of the lawsuit you cite in the last paragraph of your
letter, that is the State of Wisconsin versus the State of
Minnesota. From our reasonably extensive knowledge of American
legal matters, we are aware that any such suit between two
Sovereign States within the United States of America can only be
decided in the Supreme Court of the United States. Following a
brief review of the pending cases before the Supreme Court, the
caption of a case as you suggest is not to be found on the
current docket. Therefore, would you enlighten us as to the
particulars of this specific piece of litigation, and as to the
impact certain aspects of it would have upon your device/concept.

Secondly, while we would agree with you that the market potential
for such a product could be enormous, and possibly global in
nature, the device, as you describe it, seems to defy certain
elementary physical limitations. As a result, and before we can
pursue this matter further, we would need something by way of
rudimentary evidence that such a device could be feasibly
constructed and operated, and we would need some assurance as to
the technology that would be employed in making any such device

Reply to:
☒ CHICAGO OFFICE Three First National Plaza Suite 2300 Chicago, Illinois 60602-4205 Telephone 312.263.4141 Telecopier 312.263.1180
☐ MIAMI OFFICE 201 South Biscayne Boulevard 32nd Floor Miami, Florida 33131-2306 Telephone 305.374.2717 Telecopier 305.374.2718

61

workable. You may rest assured that our firm will treat all
information given to us in complete confidentiality, and we wo⌐
be willing, as a matter of routine and policy, to execute any
Confidentiality Agreement that you thought necessary in
connection with any rudimentary examination we may need to
perform on specific details of your device as it presently is
formulated.

Once again, I thank you for your letter to our firm regarding
this matter, and I look forward to the favor of a prompt reply
your part to our questions concerning both the legal suit you
cite and to tne issues concerning product feasibility.

Very truly yours,

William A. Brandt, Jr.

WABJr/jd

62

JAMES C. WADE III

P.O. Box 103
Montchoisi
1000 Lausanne 19
Switzerland

September 29th, 1992

Development Specialists, Inc.
Mr. William A. Brandt, Jr.
Three First National Plaza, Suite 2300
Chicago, Illinois 60602-4205, USA

Re: Speech bubbles for hearing impaired

Dear Mr. Brandt,

Thank you so much for your encouraging letter. I am happy finally
to be dealing with visionaries instead of the financial hacks one
becomes accustomed to in the inventing business.

The court case I mentioned had to do with an early test model of
the device, manufactured on the premises of the University of
Minnesota. With this particular model, the speech bubbles did not
dissolve properly and tended to float up in the air and then drift
eastwards with prevailing winds. Some of them evidently made it
as far as Wisconsin still intact. A few specimens were picked up and
analyzed by the State Environmental Protection Agency, who
unfortunately classified them in the same category as acid rain.
This little problem has since been solved, and I was very pleased
to learn from your letter that State of Wisconsin v. State of
Minnesota will not come up before the Supreme Court after all.
Perhaps in the end they settled out of court? This is good news.

As to the physical operation of the device, I would prefer not to
divulge the mechanism's workings at this stage in our discussion,
although if you are interested enough to proceed to a next phase, I
would of course send you a prototype which you could try out with
a friend in your office.

In the meantime, I'd like to tell you about three exciting new
product developments:

63

1. The device can now operate with both English and Spanish speakers. Needless to say, this opens up whole new market vistas. I am working on a German version, but it may be a while before it is ready, as the Umlauts tend to get stuck in the gearbox.

2. A Braille version for individuals who are both deaf and blind is also ready. There are still some minor problems with this model, too. The bubbles vanish too quickly for most blind people to be able to find and read them within 15 seconds.

3. Using a special muzzle attachment, the device can also be fitted over the mouth of animals so that a deaf pet-owner (or farmer) can "hear" them. The following animal-sound transliterations will be available by Christmas:

+	Woof
+	Meow
+	Baa
+	Moo
+	Oink
+	Whinny
+	Cheep
+	Quack
+	Grrrrrrrr

Again, I am looking for about $ 50 million. Can we talk?

Yours sincerely,

James Marley

PS. I believe I have met your father. He was one of the best Chancellors Germany ever had.

W. STUART WADE

3023 N. Clark Street, Box 789
Chicago, Illinois 60657

September 16th, 1992

Victoria's Secret
Attn. Product Design Dept.
P.O. Box 16590
Columbus, Ohio 43216

Re: Custom-designed lingerie

Ladies and gentlemen:

As a longtime customer of your retail shops, may I first extend
to you my congratulations on your very fine, very feminine
lingerie. I can think of no better gift to give the woman I
love at the moment.

Is it possible to order custom-made items from Victoria's Secret?
If so, I have a delicate question I would like to ask you. Could your
designers take one of your present low-cut brassiere designs and fit
it with a third cup?

I hope this might be feasible, and will supply details as soon as
I have your positive response.

Yours sincerely,

W. Stuart Wade

September 28, 1992

W. Stuart Wade
3023 North Clark St.
Box 789
Chicago, IL 60657

Dear Mr. Wade:

I am in receipt of your letter of September 16, 1992.

Victoria's Secret Catalogue offers for sale only those items
featured in our catalogues. We are a retail business, not a
manufacturing business.

Consequently, we are unable to provide you with the particular 3-
cup bra you requested.

I would like to suggest that you contact a manufacturer with your
request. You may be able to locate a company willing to design
and manufacture this specialty garment.

Sincerely,

Denise Kerkovich
Denise Kerkovich
Customer Service Specialist

JAMES C. WADE III

P.O. Box 103
Montchoisi
1000 Lausanne 19
Switzerland

May 10th, 1993

Mr. Mark Cavendish
Cavendish White
No:7, 39 Tadema Road
London SW10 OPY
England

<u>Sale of *M/Y Massarrah*</u>

Dear Mr Cavendish,

I am writing to enquire about the possible purchase of the 257-foot motor yacht you advertised for sale in the *International Herald Tribune*. I feel certain that one of my clients (a sovereign state) will find your ship of particular interest because of its large size.

Before proceeding with discussions that could lead to a sale, I first need to ask you a delicate question. Both my client and I are sensitive to the fact that great sentimental value is often attached to a sea-going vessel. In fairness to its present owner, therefore, I would like to know if you would have any objection to my client's using the *Massarrah* for gunnery or torpedo practice. As you probably know, it is almost exactly the same size as a Royal Australian Navy Wombat Class destroyer.

Please reply as soon as possible to my post office box in Lausanne, Switzerland (see address above). Many thanks in advance for your consideration.

Yours sincerely,

[signature]

CAVENDISH WHITE

YACHTING FOR THE CONNOISSEUR

CAVENDISH WHITE LTD, NUMBER SEVEN, 39 TADEMA ROAD, CHELSEA, LONDON SW10 OPY.
TELEPHONE: 071 352 6565 FAX: 071 352 6515 TELEX: 8955287 CWYOTS G.
INTERNATIONAL TELEPHONE: +44 71 352 6565 FAX: +44 71 352 6515

MC/KTG

12 May 1993

Mr James C Wade III
PO Box 103
Montchoisi
1000 Lausanne 19
SWITZERLAND

Dear Mr Wade

Re: Massarrah

Thank you for your letter of 10 May. I appreciate your comments regarding **Massarrah** and I have passed these on to the owners for their remarks. I am awaiting their reply and as soon as I have this I will of course advise you.

In the meantime please find enclosed a brochure and specification on **Massarrah**. Her asking price is US$13.5 million and she is presently lying in Palma, Mallorca, Spain where she can be inspected by arrangement. Please could you let me know if you feel your clients would be interested in her at this price level?

I look forward to hearing your comments.

Yours sincerely,

Mark Cavendish
Director

Encs

REGISTERED IN ENGLAND NO: 2442670. REGISTERED OFFICE AS ABOVE. VAT NO: 503548659.

JAMES C. WADE III

P.O. Box 103
Montchoisi
1000 Lausanne 19
Switzerland

May 17th, 1993

Mr. Mark Cavendish,
Director,
Cavendish White Ltd.
No:7, 39 Tadema Road
London SW10 0PY
England

Re: *M/Y Massarrah*

Dear Mr. Cavendish,

Thank you for your prompt reply to my query of May 10th, and
especially for the descriptive information and illustrated brochure
on the *Massarrah's* accommodations. I was quite impressed with the
extensive furnishings. Personally, I find it a shame to strip such a
beautiful yacht, but of course it makes little sense to sink her with all
her luxurious appointments intact.

Some of the equipment and fittings mentioned in your brochure do
interest me. Have you any idea what the second-hand market value
might be for the stereo system, TV's and VCR's on board?

I look forward to hearing from you with regard to my original
question.

Sincerely yours,

[signature]

CAVENDISH WHITE

YACHTING FOR THE CONNOISSEUR

CAVENDISH WHITE LTD, NUMBER SEVEN, 39 TADEMA ROAD, CHELSEA, LONDON SW10 OPY.
TELEPHONE: 071 352 6565   FAX: 071 352 6515   TELEX: 8955287 CWYOTS G.
INTERNATIONAL TELEPHONE: +44 71 352 6565 FAX: +44 71 352 6515

MC/KTG

27 May 1993

Mr James C Wade III
PO Box 103
Montchoisi
1000 Lausanne 19
SWITZERLAND

Dear Mr Wade

Re: Massarrah

Thank you for your letter of May 17th. I am sorry that I am not able to assist in advising the second hand value of on board equipment such as gyro compasses etc.

I must confess to being surprised that your principals should have any interest in purchasing **Massarrah** which is probably one of the worlds largest and most expensive private yacht for use as a torpedo target. There are many other ships of similar dimensions which could be bought for a fraction of the cost which would seem a more sensible route bearing in mind the intended use?

For instance I believe there may be several ships available from the offshore supply industry which are some 200' in length and are normally sold for between $1.5 to $3.0 million, would this not seem more sensible? If so I would be delighted to supply you with details.

I look forward to hearing from you.

Yours sincerely,

Mark Cavendish
Director

JAMES C. WADE III

P.O. Box 103
Montchoisi
1000 Lausanne 19
Switzerland

NO REPLY

June 17th, 1993

Mr. Mark Cavendish
Cavendish White
No: 7, 39 Tadema Road
London SW10 OPY
England

Sale of *M/Y Massarrah*

Dear Mr. Cavendish,

Thank you for your letter dated May 27th. I certainly couldn't fault you for not being able to answer my questions specifically. My principals and I appreciate that your own stake in this matter - 15% is the going rate, right? - forces you no doubt to focus attention on finding a buyer, rather than spending precious management time appraising the second hand value of the audio gear on board. Amazing how a couple million dollars concentrates the mind, eh?

I hope you don't mind then that I asked my agent in Palma to check this issue out locally. He reports that he managed to slip aboard and says that the equipment in question is in pretty good shape, although one of the stereo speakers in the main deck sitting room, just off the owner's double cabin, hisses too much. He suspects the woofer needs replacing. Incidentally, my man also reports a clogged toilet in the yellow guest cabin on the lower deck.

(Though I don't want to be presumptuous, the thought occurs to me that you may want to review your security procedures while you're at it.)

Thank you for your kind offer of the names of other, less expensive, target ships. After consulting with my client, I am pleased to inform you that they have had a good look through your lavish brochure on the vessel and have become downright *eager* to sink her, as they believe there is a good deal of public relations benefit to be squeezed out of the story, particularly if it can be carried live on CNN - as I'm sure it can be if we drop the right name here and there. So it truly behooves us now to find out how your principals would feel about this. I very much look forward to your reply.

Sincerely yours,

[signature]

71

W. STUART WADE

3023 N. Clark Street, No. 789
Chicago, Illinois 60657

October 15th, 1993

Prentice Hall Publishing Co.
Cookbook Division
15 Columbus Circle
New York NY 10023

Dear sirs,

For about 150 years my family has passed down recipes from one generation to the next, and I would like to publish them. I have two reasons. First, I truly believe that these recipes are the key to some of the most delicious meals on this earth. Second (a personal wish), I would like to honor the memory of my great-grandmother, who collected them all on 800 yellowing but meticulously inscribed index cards. She died last month of stomach cancer.

Cooking with Tobacco will be unlike any other cookbook on the market. I should probably mention right off the bat that it is not only for smokers! Alas, when tobacco is mentioned these days, most non-users think only of the fumes. *Cooking with Tobacco* will help overcome these prejudices. For beginners, it will show you how to use tobacco as a garnish, main course, seasoning, salad, meat tenderizer, rhubarb substitute, mouth-watering dessert, refreshing beverage, and even a beautiful table centerpiece.

Most people don't know that tobacco cuisine has a long and rich history going all the way back to Plymouth Rock. Did you know for example that at the first Thanksgiving, the Indians taught the Pilgrims how to French fry tobacco to make a bubble gum chaw? I can add lots of fascinating anecdotes like this.

Finally, for those who already love the taste of tobacco, there will be a plethora of new ideas, among them: tobacco chips, blueberry tobacco muffins, Red Man salad, tobacco pancakes, Borkum Riff spaghetti sauce, and many others.

I am sure this book will be a tremendous success if it sells well, and I would like to know if you would consider being the lucky publisher. Looking forward to hearing from you,

Yours,

W. Stuart Wade

PRENTICE HALL

Paramount Publishing Consumer Group
15 Columbus Circle
New York, NY 10023
212-373-8500
Fax: 212-373-8642

General Reference Division

November 19, 1993

Mr. W. Stuart Wade
3023 North Clark Street #789
Chicago, IL 60657

Dear Mr. Wade,

We received your letter proposing to write <u>Cooking with
Tobacco</u>. While it sounds like an interesting (and
unusual!) topic, it does not fit in our line of books.
Good luck with the project.

Sincerely,

Rachel Simon
Associate Editor

Enclosure

A Paramount Communications Company

JAMES C. WADE III

P.O. Box 103
Montchoisi
CH - 1000 Lausanne 19
Switzerland

April 12th 1992

Consulate of Panama
Rue de Lausanne 72
1202 Geneva
Switzerland

Dear sirs,

I am planning a trip to Central America next year with my family, and we would like to spend two or three weeks backpacking in Panama.

In the course of my trip preparations, however, I read the memoirs of the late Prof. Hullington McDowell, who visited Panama some thirty years ago. His book has raised serious doubts in my mind about the safety of Panamanian jungles for my children.

According to Professor McDowell's account, one evening he heard some scuffling noises outside his tent and when he went to investigate, he discovered three mosquitos trying to drag his two-year-old son into the underbrush. Thinking fast, he fired his pistol into the air, which scared them into dropping the boy and flying away. In spite of the bad light and their erratic escape flight, the Professor was able to get off three more shots, mortally wounding one and winging another. The next morning he retrieved the corpse of the dead mosquito. He claimed it was fourteen inches long and weighed over 3 lbs. Even in metric terms, that is pretty big.

I too will be travelling with young children (Birchley, age three, and Constance, age fourteen months), and I would frankly be very disappointed were this to happen to either of them.

Could you please assure me that you have eradicated such insects? If not satisfied that my children can spend time safely near some stagnant Panamanian watering hole, we may have to reconsider our plans and go back to Colonial Williamsburg...again.

Many thanks in advance for your reply.

Yours sincerely,

Consulado General de Panamá

Nouvelle adresse :
72, rue de Lausanne
1202 Genève
Tél. 738 03 88

Geneva, April 15, 1992

Dear Sir:

I could not help laughing when I read your letter dated 12-4-92.

How anyone, like Prof. McDowell, could have written about such strain of mosquitos in any part of the world? How could anyone believe such fiction?

I recommend that you consult an elementary book on entomology.

Yours truly,

Dr. Osvaldo Velásquez
General Consul

Mr. James C. Wade
P.O. Box 103
Montchoisi
1000 Lausanne 19

3023 N. Clark Street, No. 789
Chicago, Illinois 60657

August 14th, 1992

Ben & Jerry's Homemade Ice Cream
P.O. Box 240
Waterbury, Vermont 05676

Dear Ben and Jerry,

Your great concern for the fate of the human race has not gone unnoticed. I admire your corporation's activism and would like to tell you about a movement that may also interest you.

"EcoPet" is only in its genesis, but it will be a non-profit foundation devoted to raising worldwide consciousness about the necessity of collecting and recycling domestic animal waste.

Many people don't realize that dog and cat feces contains virtually the same chemical elements as many fossil fuels. The same goes for rabbit, hamster, canary, and especially turtle feces. If properly amassed and reformulated, a year's worth of feces from just 500 dogs and cats could generate sufficient power to heat every home in a city the size of Evansville, Indiana for one hour and ten minutes.

Today, this would not be cheap: we do not have the infrastructure to do the job right. But refecenation technology already exists - we just have to have the national will to invest in it. The governments of France, Norway, Lesotho, Papua New Guinea, and Kiribati have already launched refecenation programs, but the United States continues to drag its feet (so to speak).

I would like to extend an invitation to you both to be spokesmen for our efforts in America. It is only through creating public awareness and raising significant investment funds that the process of refecenation can be made affordable to all. At EcoPet, we foresee a day when all pet owners will buy our heavily marketed recycling containers, collect their pets' waste, and bask in the glow of environmentally sound energy creation.

Won't you join our other potential spokespersons Gary Hart, Joan Baez, and Crown Prince Narahito of Japan in this historic effort? I look forward to receiving your reply.

Yours sincerely,

W. Stuart Wade

PS. For our files, what are your last names?

BEN&JERRY'S®

VERMONT'S FINEST • ICE CREAM & FROZEN YOGURT™

ROUTE 100, P.O. BOX 240, WATERBURY, VERMONT 05676

October 22, 1992

Mr. W. Stuart Wade
3023 N. Clark Street
Box 789
Chicago, IL 60657

Dear Mr. Wade:

Thank you for your letter of August 14th. Please accept our apologies for taking so long to respond. We have enclosed some free pint coupons to make amends.

While we appreciate your invitation to have Ben and Jerry represent your organization, EcoPet, we must decline due to the many commitments that we have with our own in-house social mission efforts. We are currently focusing on our Leave No Child Behind campaign with the Children's Defense Fund.

Thank you very much for your interest and for your support. We wish you all the best with your worthwhile efforts. May all of your future endeavors be successful.

Sincerely,

Cindi LaDeau
Consumer Affairs

Enc: (2) Free Pint Coupons

WATERBURY FACTORY
PHONE: (802) 244-5641
FAX: (802) 244-8081

COMPANY OFFICES
PHONE: (802) 244-6957
FAX: (802) 244-5944

♻ Printed on Recycled Paper

ADMINISTRATION
PHONE: (802) 244-6957
FAX: (802) 244-1175

P.O. Box 103
Montchoisi
1000 Lausanne 19
July 11th, 1992

Swatch AG
SMH New Product Development Center
Attn. Mr. Nicholas Hayek, President,
P.O. Box 3256
2500 Bienne 3, Switzerland

Dear Mr. Hayek,

I read not too long ago that you are introducing a Swatch Car and would soon be looking for new, environmentally friendly materials to build it with. May I suggest that you take a serious look at <u>animal cartilage</u>? Not only is cartilage strong, resilient, and lightweight; it could even act as its own shock absorber.

Cartilage would be very cheap to acquire, since it has no other industrial applications that I know of and is even considered by most meat packers as something to be discarded. Therefore, thanks to volume discounts, I'm sure that you could get your hands on all the cartilage you would need to produce several thousand car bodies a year for much less than the price of steel, chrome, or even plastic - just the thing to keep those budget weenies in your company happy.

Furthermore, the whitish-yellowish color of unpainted cartilage could help in establishing brand recognition for the Swatch Car, just as the burnished stainless steel body helped create the snazzy image of the DeLorean. The only downside risk I can see is that people may start calling the Swatch Car by some disparaging nickname, like "Gristlemobile." However, as with all your other products, the price/quality relationship would soon put an end to such idle chatter.

My brother Stuart lives in Chicago, meat-packing capital of the western world. Should I get him to start asking around for prices for you?

Yours sincerely,

[signature]

PS. By the way, I bet other meat by-products could make good components in the Swatch Car, too. Have you ever thought about using spleen instead of foam as an inexpensive seat filler?

Rue de Boujean 9
Case postale 3256
CH-2500 Bienne 3
Téléphone 032 277 377
Téléfax 032 277 321

Une division de Tissot S.A.
A company of SMH

Mr. James C. Wade III
P.O. Box 103
Montchoisi

1000 Lausanne 19

Bienne, September 4th, 1992
DB/jt

Dear Mr. Wade,

We thank you for your letter to Mr. Hayek concerning animal cartilage and spleen.

We read with interest your original proposal; however we are sorry to inform you that we have already defined our concepts and our partners in the fields:

- vehicle structure
- seat filler

We thank you for your interest in our project.

Sincerely,

CENTRE DEVELOPPEMENT
NOUVEAUX PRODUITS SMH

D. Berdoz

Copy: Mr. N.G.Hayek

W. STUART WADE

3023 N. Clark Street, No. 789
Chicago, Illinois 60657

July 14th, 1992

Dep Corporation
2101 East Via Arado
Rancho Dominguez, California 90220

<u>Attn. Product Manager, hair gel</u>

Dear sir or madam,

I am a big fan of your Dep extra super hold hair gel. I often wear my hair in rather demanding convex arrangements at my day job (I'm an attorney), and only Dep can meet the challenge.

Reading the fine print on the bottle one day last week, I was surprised to see that it says "Dep is not animal tested." If you don't want to try out Dep on animals, I guess that's your own business, but I just wanted to let you know that I've done it, and it works just fine on them, too. My afghan Lars enjoys having his fur spiked and blow-dried - he looks just like a miniature (and more svelte) stegosaurus. My cats Sid and Nancy also seem to like it when I "lionize" them.

Between the three of them, they have only thrown up once, so I would say it's pretty safe to do animal testing with the stuff.

I just thought you would want to know.

All the best,

W. Stuart Wade

DEPCORPORATION

August 20, 1992

Stuart Wade
3023 North Clark Street
Chicago, IL 60657

RE: Dep Super Hold Gel

Dear Stuart:

Thank you for your letter telling us of your pleasant experience with the above product.

Comments and inquiries from our consumers are always appreciated as it helps us to market better products.

Thank you once again for your interest, and support, of our products.

Enclosed is a coupon to use on your next purchase of a Dep product.

Sincerely,

M. Reede

Marsha Reede
Consumer Services Coordinator

/mr

Enclosure: Dep Coupons

JAMES C. WADE III

P.O. Box 103
Montchoisi
1000 Lausanne 19
Switzerland

September 7th, 1992

Nobel Prize Nomination Committee
Stockholm
Sweden

Dear sirs,

I would like to nominate Dr. Hamilton Fung for the Nobel Prize in Chemistry, but I'm not really sure how to go about it. I wonder if you could pop a nomination form in the mail to me?

Just out of curiosity - may I ask exactly what level of achievement you are looking for? I imagine your expectations are fairly high for prizewinners. I'm not quite sure if Dr. Fung's work is up your alley (he has been working on an artificial cottage cheese.) Do nominees have to answer some kind of a checklist, for example:

Breakthrough?   yes ____   no ____
Helped mankind?   yes ____   no ____   not sure ____

It's hard to guess how Fung's work would be judged from the humanitarian point of view, but let me tell you, he could certainly use some of those much-revered simoleons.

Thank you very much for taking the time to consider my questions. I am looking forward to hearing from you with the appropriate forms to fill out.

Yours sincerely,

James Wade

NOBELSTIFTELSEN

The Nobel Foundation

▪

September 15, 1992.

Mr. James C. Wade III
P.O. Box 103
Montchoisi
1000 Lausanne 19
Switzeröand

Dear Sir,

    Referring to your letter of September 7 concerning
nominating a friend of yours Dr. Hamilton Fung, for the Nobel
Prize in Chemistry we want to inform you that the Nobel
Foundation is only the administrative body for the Nobel Prizes
and has no influence on the awarding of the Prizes. The
activities of the Nobel Foundation and the Nobel Committees are
laid down in the Statutes of The Nobel Foundation. We regret to
tell you that the Nobel Committees only treat questions
relating to works of candidates for a Nobel Prize which are
submitted according to the statutes.
It has to be pointed out that the right to nominate the
candidates is reserved for certain categories, indicated in the
enclosed list.

Sincerely yours,

Kristina Fallenius
Information Department

Encl.

Mailing address: Box 5232, S-102 45 Stockholm, Sweden
Street address: Sturegatan 14
Telephone: (+46 8) 663 09 20 Telex: 12382 Nobhaus S

83

3023 N. Clark Street, No. 789
Chicago, Illinois 60657
September 30th, 1992

Mr. Charlton Heston
8730 Sunset Boulevard
Los Angeles, California 90069

Dear Mr. Heston,

I would like to invite you to a party organized by my brother James
and myself in honor of the 75th birthday of Prof. Törpör Oligops. The
party will be held on Saturday, April 24th, 1993, in the Grand Casino
at the Château du Bison Futé in Lausanne, Switzerland.

As an actor, you are surely familiar with some of the work of Prof.
Oligops, who spent nearly a third of his adult life among the nomads of
the Gobi, noting their fascinating and bizarre marital practices. His
richly illustrated anthropology textbook, *The Swollen Uplands,* published forty years ago, became a surprise best-seller and was even
made into a Broadway musical, called "A Whiff of Leather," starring
Vince Pomeroy as Admiral Halsey.

The Professor always believed that a movie version of his book was
bound to be made, and he never wavered in his opinion that you would
have been the best possible man in the role of Fritz, the demented
bridegroom. He admires you very much, and has often said that thinking about your many talents helped keep him sane during his long iso-
lation in the desert.

We are hoping that Ringo Starr will be there to lead us in singing
Happy Birthday to the Professor, and we would be honored if you
could also join us on this very special occasion. Would you be so kind
as to let us know if you will be able to come, by confirming to my
brother James Wade at the following address: P.O. Box 103, 1000
Lausanne 19, Switzerland.

On behalf of Prof. Oligops, I hope to see you next April 24th!
With very cordial wishes,

Yours sincerely,

W. Stuart Wade

PS. Could you also let us know whether you'd be able to make it to
the grill-out on Sunday at David Bowie's place? Thanks!

CHARLTON HESTON

October 15, 1992

Dear Mr. Wade:

Thanks for the invitation to join you
for the 75th birthday of Prof. Torpor Oligops
you're having in Switzerland in April: it was
good of you to think of me. I'm certain it
will be a memorable event for all those
attending.

Unhappily, I expect to be doing a film
in April and thus not able to attend. I hope
you and Prof. Oligops will accept instead my
best wishes for a wonderful occasion and Many
Happy Returns of the day!

Cordially,

JAMES C. WADE III

P.O. Box 103
Montchoisi
1000 Lausanne 19
Switzerland

August 26th, 1992

The National Library of Poetry
PO Box 704
Owings Mills, Maryland 21117
USA

Dear sirs and madams,

I understand you have just announced a poetry contest, and I would like to enter the following poem, which I have written in honor of my host country, Switzerland:

Thoughts on a Boulder

O alpine meadows
sun rising over misty stream
monkeys monkeys monkeys
let peace find a haven
in craggy crags
of big mountains
of neutrality

Clouds sweep by
I am lost in thought
of my many-bladed knife
one is a corkscrew
monkeys monkeys monkeys
bank accounts in desolation

O small land of high altitudes!
Cows graze sullenly munching
monkeys monkeys monkeys
let me down from here,
won't you please, Dave?

Looking forward to hearing from you regarding the prize money, etc.,

James Wade

The National Library of Poetry

11419-10 Cronridge Drive • Post Office Box 704 • Owings Mills, Maryland 21117 • (410) 356-2000

September 30, 1992

James Wade III
PO Box 103
1000 Lausanne 19
Montchoisi
SWITZERLAND

Dear James,   *[Re: O Alpine meadows sun rising over . . .]*

It is my pleasure to inform you that, after reading and discussing your poem, our Selection Committee has certified your poem as a semi-finalist in our 1992 North American Open Poetry Contest. Your poem will automatically be entered into the final competition, held in Fall 1992. As a semi-finalist, you have an excellent chance of winning one of 70 cash or gift prizes--you may even win the $1000.00 Grand Prize (a complete list of prizes can be found on one of the enclosures to this letter).

IMAGINE YOUR POEM . . . PUBLISHED IN A BEAUTIFUL ANTHOLOGY!

And James, in view of your talent, we also wish to publish your poem in our forthcoming anthology Where Dreams Begin (Library of Congress ISBN 1-56167-038-3).

Where Dreams Begin

Library of Congress ISBN 1-56167-039-1

Where Dreams Begin, scheduled for publication in Fall 1992 will be a classic, edition-quality hardbound volume--printed on fine milled paper to last for generations. It will make a handsome addition to any library, a treasured family keepsake, or a highly valued personal gift. And best of all . . . it will feature a poem by James Wade III!

NO OBLIGATION WHATSOEVER

Before going any further, let me make one thing clear . . . your poem was selected for publication, and as a contest semi-finalist, solely on the basis of merit. You are under no obligation whatsoever to submit any entry fee, any subsidy payment, or to make any purchase of any kind. Of course, many people do wish to own a copy of the publication in which their artistry appears. If this is the case, we welcome your order--and guarantee your satisfaction. Please see the enclosed material for special discount information if you are interested in owning a copy of Where Dreams Begin.

SO, WHAT HAPPENS NOW?

As I mentioned above, your poem has automatically been entered in the final competition--so you need take no action on the contest at this time. However, regarding the publication of your poem, you must complete the enclosed Author's Release stating that the

[and the packet went on and on...]

JAMES C. WADE III

P.O. Box 103
Montchoisi
1000 Lausanne 19
Switzerland

October 12th, 1992

The National Library of Poetry
Mr. Howard Ely, Managing Editor
5 Gwynns Mill Court
POB 704
Owings Mills, Maryland 21117
USA

Dear Mr. Ely,

I cannot tell you how excited I was to get your letter and find out that my poem will be included in your beautifully entitled anthology "Where Dreams Begin." Enclosed is my order form, biographical info, and money.

The only other time my work has been in print was six years ago, when I had a short story published in a book called "Changing Tastes in Mediocrity." It was a spoof on the margarine business. If you are interested in prose, I could send you a copy.

But inclusion in your book means so much more to me than that first publication, and I want to thank you. It is not an easy thing to hold a full-time job and write poetry on the side, especially if you're like me and like to watch a lot of TV. Getting your letter was the most encouraging thing that has happened to me in a long, a very long, o! a very very long time.

Thank you!

Sincerely,

[signature]

The National Library of Poetry

11419-10 Cronridge Drive • Post Office Box 704 • Owings Mills, Maryland 21117 • (410) 356-2000

BIOGRAPHICAL DATA FORM

We are glad to be able to make your biographical profile available to the public and the media in a **special biographical section.** We must charge a nominal fee ($20) for the added costs of preparing and printing your biographical profile, however you are in no way obligated to include this information—your poem will still be published without your profile.

Instructions: Complete this form only if you wish to have your biography appear in the publication. Please answer only those items that you want to include in your profile. You may leave any item blank. **Please include $20 for the added cost of this service.**

Please print or type

Name James C. Wade III

Pen name(s) Hogarth Rodriguez

Date of birth Dec. 31, 1959 (last of an era)

Place of birth Two Buttes, Montana

Parents James C. Wade, Jr. and Sue Armstrong-Jones Wade

Spouse Heidi

Date of marriage October 8, 1988

Children Free, Jan 30, 1988, Arthur, Jan. 30, 1988 (twins)

Education O. Henry High School, University of Montana, Henderson State Vocational College (Hair Styling)

Occupation Wind tunnel administrator

Memberships Lausanne YMCA, Swiss-American Poetry Exchange, Glee Club, Neo-Vulgarians Gourmet Club

Honors and Awards 1982 "Keep America Tidy" Runner-up; 1986 Best New Fiction in "Changing Tastes in Mediocrity"

SAMPLE BIOGRAPHY

LIEBKNECHT, MICHELLE
Pen name: Pat Munter; *Born:* December 11, 1958; Baltimore, MD; *Parents:* David Gill, Dolores Gill; *Spouse:* Patrick Liebknecht; February 26, 1987; *Children:* Timothy Wayne, Jeffrey Scott; *Education:* Franklin High, Villa Julie College; *Occupation:* Math teacher, North Point Elementary School, Baltimore, MD; *Memberships:* American Heart Association, Trinity Lutheran Church Scholarship Committee; *Honors:* Delta Kappa Gamma, Dean's list; *Other writings:* Several poems published in local newspapers, article for *The Saturday Evening Post*; *Personal note:* I strive to reflect the goodness of mankind in my writing. I have been greatly influenced by the early romantic poets.; *Address:* Reisterstown, MD 21136

Other writings (unpublished): "Crucible of Mange" "The Confessions of Yuri Gagarin" "Sparring with Hegel and Kant" "The Goddess of Vegetation" "Swine Flu and You" (pamphlet)

Personal note or philosophical statement
Although I live abroad, my writing is quintessentially American in its struggle with truth and realism. Also: I was deeply touched by Maastricht.

Address P.O. Box 103, Montchoisi, 1000 Lausanne 19, Switzerland

☒ Include my complete address in my profile.
☐ Include only my city and state in my profile.

Signature

The National Library of Poetry

11419-10 Cronridge Drive • Post Office Box 704 • Owings Mills, Maryland 21117 • (410) 356-2000

James Wade III
PO Box 103
1000 Lausanne 19
Montchoisi
SWITZERLAND

Dear James,

Thank you for your entry in our recent contest. Your poem was recognized by the judges as being among the best 3% of all entries judged. We are therefore pleased to award you our Editor's Choice Award for your contest entry as published in <u>Where Dreams Begin</u>. Congratulations on your significant achievement.

Sincerely,

The National Library of Poetry

Editor's Choice Award

Presented to

James Wade III

for Outstanding Achievement in Poetry
Presented By
The National Library of Poetry
1993

Cynthia Stevens
Editor

Caroline Sullivan
Editor

W. STUART WADE

3023 N. Clark Street, No. 789
Chicago, Illinois 60657

November 20th, 1992

House of Seagram
Attn. Advertising Manager, Gordon's Gin
800 Third Avenue
New York, New York 10022

Dear Sir or Madam:

May I ask you some questions regarding your print advertising techniques? I teach a course in advertising to an adult education class at the Discover© Urban Nighttime Chicago Education center (DUNCE)™. I hope I am not intruding, but I often use examples of really effective ads in my lectures, and I like to go straight to the source for my teaching information.

This semester we have been studying subliminal messages, and I wondered if you could tell us from your own experience which of the following images work best for you in airbrushed glamour shots of Gordon's gin on ice:

Medusas, Griffins, etc.	Crosses (upright or inverted)
A pair of menacing eyes	The words "lust", "drink",
Breasts (singly or in sets?)	"Satan", or "Godiva"
Handcuffs	Pelicans
	Snakes, trains, salamis, etc.

Another question. Is there one individual in your company who is responsible for coming up with these hidden symbols, or are they arrived at by brainstorming in groups? My class is very interested in learning about this creative process, and we thought that perhaps you would like to come to Chicago once and speak to us on how this is done. In class exercises, I have found that small groups come up with much better subliminal ideas than students working alone. For example, one group thought a shampoo ad should include the words *"marriage contract"* hidden in the model's hair, which you have to admit is pretty good for beginners.

I look forward to your reply.

Sincerely yours,

W. Stuart Wade

UNITED
DISTILLERS

December 14, 1992

Mr. W. Stuart Wade
3032 North Clark Street, #789
Chicago, IL 60657

Dear Mr. Wade:

Your letter of November 20 sent to Gordon's Gin at Schenley
Industries has just made it to my attention.

Schenley Industries has been consolidated into United Distillers
Glenmore based in Stamford, Connecticut which explains the delay.

As to your letter regarding Gordon's advertising practices. We do
not employ any "subliminal advertising techniques, nor do we
"airbrush" any "glamour shots".

We hope that this satisfies your query for information.

Sincerely,

Jane Birnbaum
Vice President Corporate Communications

W. STUART WADE

3023 N. Clark Street, No. 789
Chicago, Illinois 60657

January 5th, 1993

United Distillers North America, Inc.
Ms Jane Birnbaum,
Vice President, Corporate Communications
Six Landmark Square
Stamford, Connecticut 06901-2704

Dear Ms. Birnbaum,

Many thanks for your letter of December 14th. My apologies for
the late reply - in fact I was quite busy in the last few weeks
preparing my presentation to the annual Chicago Subliminal
Advertising Symposium. I thought there was a chance I might
meet you there, but no such luck.

Please be assured that I am well aware of the Code of Silence on
subliminal techniques, and I fully understand your response
denying the use of airbrush modification. I'm sure I would do the
same if I were in your shoes. In a rush to dash off my previous
letter to you, I forgot to mention my operative name: please forgive
the oversight; it is "Haskell 631". This might have eased your
suspicions. (I am also listed in the '92 *Sublimicon* - if you check your
copy, you'll see that it confirms my area of specialty as ice cubes.)

My students and I are only interested in gaining the benefits of
your expertise, not in exposing anything to the public at large.
If you would like to fly in and speak to my class, I'm sure we
can arrange it. It goes without saying that your identity would
be protected. Think it over and get back to me!

Sincerely,

W. Stuart Wade

PS. Very nice touch on your last Gordon's ad: I very nearly missed
the cloaked figure in the upper left quadrant!

3023 N. Clark Street, No. 789
Chicago, Illinois 60657

January 27th, 1993

Alexander Graham Bell Association for the Deaf
3417 Volta Place Northwest
Washington, D.C. 20007

DEAR SIRS:

CAN'T YOU DO ANYTHING ABOUT MAKING
PUBLIC PHONES LOUDER? I CAN HARDLY HEAR
A DAMN THING!

YOURS,

W. Stuart Wade

International Hearing Society

formerly the National Hearing Aid Society
20361 Middlebelt Road • Livonia, Michigan 48152
Telephone: 313/478-2610 • Facsimile: 313/478-4520

February 8, 1993

Mr. W. Stuart Wade
3023 N. Clark Street, #789
Chicago, Illinois 60657

Dear Mr. Clark:

Thank you for your letter of January 27th. Please note that the name of this association is now the International Hearing Society.

Telephone access for the hearing impaired has long been a priority. In 1988 the Congress took a giant step in this direction with the enactment of the Hearing Aid Compatibility Act (P.L. 100-394). Aspects of the Americans with Disabilities Act (P.L. 101-336) further bolster the rights of the hearing impaired.

Self Help for Hard of Hearing People (SHHH) has been perhaps the loudest voice for the rights of the hearing impaired. You may wish to contact them at 7800 Wisconsin Avenue, Bethesda, Maryland 20814, concerning their advocacy efforts.

We appreciate your interest and thank you again for contacting the International Hearing Society.

Sincerely,

J. Lovell sls

James P. Lovell
Government Relations Director

JPL:sls

42nd Annual Convention
September 1 - 5, 1993
San Diego Marriott

95

JAMES C. WADE III

P.O. Box 103
Montchoisi
1000 Lausanne 19
Switzerland

August 3rd, 1992

Spot Satellite Image Corp.
1897 Preston White Drive
Reston, Virginia 22091
USA

Dear sirs,

Is it true that satellite photography has become so advanced that nowadays you can pick out earthly details down to the size of a baked potato?

If this is the case, I have a request to make. On Saturday, July 17th, 1993, a friend of mine is going to be getting married in New Harmony, Indiana (38°08' N, 87°57' W). The reception will be taking place at The Red Geranium, in the middle of town.

Would it be possible for one of your satellites to pass by and take a picture of the bridal couple and all the guests? When the satellite is due to fly over New Harmony, we would all step out onto the restaurant's patio, look up at the sky, and wave. The reception starts at 6 p.m., so any time after that would be fine. We just need to know the exact time the satellite will be overhead.

In case they don't like the first shot, how long would we have to wait till the satellite is back in position for a retake?

Many thanks in advance for letting me know if this will work, and how much it will cost.

Sincerely yours,

[signature]

PS. We would prefer a natural-color photo, rather than one of those heat-sensitive jobs that would make us all look dark red and green. Thank you.

JAMES C. WADE III

P.O. Box 103
Montchoisi
1000 Lausanne 19
Switzerland

August 31st, 1992

Spot Satellite Image Corp.
1897 Preston White Drive
Reston, Virginia 22091
USA

Dear sirs,

I received your brochure in the mail this morning and would like
to thank you for sending it to me. All that technical information
about your satellites is certainly interesting, but it didn't shed any
light at all on what time the wedding party should be stepping out-
doors and flashing our pearly whites up at Spot. (How did you come
up with this name, by the way? Sounds like a large, friendly dog.)

For obvious reasons, we don't want to stand there all evening staring
at the sky with big stupid grins frozen on our faces, so we really need
to pin down the time when the satellite will actually be taking our
picture. The best time for us would be about 7 p.m. since the band
is supposed to start at half past and everybody will want to go in and
start dancing.

Do you have some kind of overnight developing service? It would
be great if Ricki and Bobbi Sue could get their picture by the
following weekend (July 24th), which is the date they'll be returning
from their honeymoon in the Poconos.

Last question: I need to know how much it will cost, please. If it's
more than a hundred bucks, we'll have to pass the hat.

Thanks for your help,

Yours,

[signature]

SPOT
Image
Corporation

1897
Preston
White
Drive

Reston,
Virginia
22091-4368

703/
620-2200
Fax 703/
648-1813

James C. Wade
P.O. Box 103
Montchoisi
1000 Lausanne 19
Switzerland

23 September 1992

Dear Mr. Wade:

Thank you for your continued interest in SPOT Image. Enclosed is a sheet which describes our ground resolution capabilites. I have highlighted some information on that page, for your information. The smallest object that we can view is the size of half a tennis court. If you are interested in actually stepping outside and being seen in the image, we do not have the capability, nor does any other civilian satellite system. However, may I make a suggestion...aerial photography

I am also enclosing I am sending a fee scedule with the price of the product you would be interested in highlighted, this cost is $950. A fee of $600 would be charged to program the satellite to aquire an image at that particular time. In addition $1,500 would be charged for rush fees if you want it within two weeks of the date it was aquired. The total cost of this product would be $3,000.

As for how we got our name, SPOT. It stands for Satellite Pour l'Observation de la Terre (French for Satellite for observing the Earth).

Again, thank you for your interest in SPOT Image. Please give us a call if you have any other questions.

Sincerely,

Kim Sunderland

Kim Sunderland
Sales Support

JAMES C. WADE III

P.O. Box 103
Montchoisi
1000 Lausanne 19
Switzerland

August 30th, 1993

PTT Post-Telephone-Telegraph
General Directorate - Business Development Section
Viktoriastrasse 21
3030 Bern, Switzerland

Dear sirs,

You may have heard of the so-called "capsule hotels" which are popular in Japan. Instead of getting a room, guests check themselves into a big pull-out drawer in the wall, which has a bed, TV, and some other amenities inside.

Would you be interested in jointly developing a similar idea with me here in Switzerland, converting some of your prime-location telephone booths into a hotel chain?

At present, of course, your phone booths are not adequately furnished to function as hotel rooms, and they would have to be re-outfitted to bring them up to acceptable comfort levels. First, I foresee adding a vertical divider creating two separate "rooms" out of each booth. One would be a pleasantly padded compartment for upright sleeping (which doctors recommend as the best way to sleep, by the way), while the other half would contain a telephone (already present), mini-bar, shower, etc.

By now you have surely realized the key element that makes this hotel concept even better than the Japanese idea: with the "Booth Hotel," you are giving the traveller an exceptionally wide choice of locations for his overnight stay. By calling a toll-free reservation hot-line, he can find out about dozens of available booths in the area where he wants to stay. He can pick a booth right around the corner from his business appointments the next day, or he can stay in a quiet suburban train station or a leafy green park - it's up to the customer.

Needless to say, "Booth Hotels" would be an excellent new business for you, because it turns your phone booths - normally pretty moribund pieces of real estate - into real revenue producers.

Looking forward to meeting you and working out the financing,

Yours sincerely,

[signature]

Ihr Zeichen
Votre référence
Vostro riferimento

Ihre Nachricht vom
Votre communication du
Vostra comunicazione del

Unser Zeichen
Notre référence
Nostro riferimento

Rückruf
Rappel
Richiamare

Datum
Date 7/9/93
Data

Telefon 031 62 11 11   GENERAL DIRECTORATE OF SWISS PTT   **TELECOM** ✠
Telefax 031 62 64 78   **Residential Customers**
Telex 901 046 gdtg ch Güterstrasse 24/26
Postkonto 30-320-6   3030 Bern
Telegramm   Gentel

Mr James C. Wade III
P.O. Box 103
Montchoisi
1000 Lausanne 19

Dear Mr Wade

Thank you for your letter of 30 August outlining your proposal to turn telephone booths into hotel accommodation.

The PTT's scope of activities is defined in the PTT Organization Act of 6 October 1960 as the provision of postal and telecommunication services. There is however no legal basis or authority for running other types of service, including the provision of converted public phone booths as sleeping accomodation. That is why we cannot, unfortunately, consider your scheme.

Sincerely,

Business Area Residential Customers
The Assistant:

A. Känzig

PK / Febr. 93

JAMES C. WADE III

P.O. Box 103
Montchoisi
1000 Lausanne 19
Switzerland

May 10th, 1993

Purdue University
Dept. of Physical Education
West Lafayette, Indiana 47907
USA

Dear sirs,

After a hiatus of 15 years, I would like to finish my bachelor's degree. Unfortunately I had to quit my studies early because of a medical problem (bifurcated torso, long since corrected).

All my accumulated college credit is from various U.S. universities, but as you can see from my return address, I live abroad now. I suppose this means that if I am to complete an American degree, my work will have to be through a correspondence course.

For a long time I thought this was impossible in my particular area of study, Physical Education and Bodybuilding. Then I saw your ad "Learn Karate by Mail and Earn College Credit" in last week's issue of *Underachievers Monthly Digest*. I was very excited about your claim that a black belt, plus 10 Purdue credit hours, are "only as far away as your mailbox."

I really feel that a bachelor's degree is at last within my grasp! Could you please send me an application as soon as possible? I look forward to hearing from you soon.

Yours sincerely,

James Wade

PURDUE UNIVERSITY

DEPARTMENT OF HEALTH,
KINESIOLOGY, AND LEISURE STUDIES

May 19, 1993

Mr. James C. Wade III
P.O. Box 103
Montchoisi
1000 Lausanne 19
Switzerland

Dear Mr. Wade,

Purdue University does not offer college credit via correspondence in any health or physical education courses. Did the add mention Purdue University?

Please write again if we can be of any assistance.

Sincerely,

Don L. Corrigan
Interim Department Head

DLC:ko

1362 LAMBERT • WEST LAFAYETTE, IN 47907-1362 • (317) 494-3177 • FAX (317) 496-1239

W. STUART WADE

3023 N. Clark Street, No. 789
Chicago, Illinois 60657
USA

October 8th, 1992

Heineken Breweries NV
Attn. Business Development Manager
P.O. Box 28
NL - 1000 AA Amsterdam
Netherlands

Dear sir or madam,

Heineken played a formative role in my adolescence, and I would like to return the favor, so to speak, by sharing an idea with you that I think could cement Heineken's place as the world's preeminent brewski, in the next century and beyond.

My idea has to do with the way Heineken is bottled. Instead of using glass bottles or cans, why not sell Heineken in "bottles" made of pretzels? You would open the bottle by biting off the top and eating it. Then you would take a swig of beer, and continue like this, eating and drinking your way to the bottom of the bottle.

This idea solves the problem of recycling, faced not only by Heineken drinkers but by all of mankind in general. It also provides a service to all your loyal drinkers who otherwise would have to buy their beer and pretzels separately, sometimes even from separate vendors in completely different physical locations! Imagine the popularity of this innovation at baseball games or at the beach. Or among people with only one hand free!

Please don't ask to compensate me for this idea, even though you may think it a stroke of genius. I would personally spearhead the market assault for you in the U.S., and look forward to your reply.

Yours sincerely,

W. Stuart Wade

HEINEKEN INTERNATIONAAL BEHEER B.V.

Correspondence-address:
P.O. Box 28
1000 AA Amsterdam Netherlands
Cables Operations Amsterdam
Telephone (20) 5 23 92 39
Telex 10501
Telecopier (20) 6 26 35 03

Mr. W.S. Stuart
3023 North Clark Street 789
Chicago, Il 60657
U.S.A.

Your ref.	Our ref.	Direct line: No.	Amsterdam
	FT/JR	5 239 225	October 16, 1992

Dear Mr. Wade,

Thank you for your recent letter with regard to your idea.

We appreciate the fact that you wanted to share your idea with us. Although your idea would solve the recycling problem it is unfortunately not possible to have a liquid subsuance in bottles made of pretzels.

Please find enclosed a small souvenir as a token of our appreciation. Thank you again for writing us and we remain, with kind regards,

Yours sincerely,

Ms. F.N. Tjaarda
Director of Corporate Public Relations

Office-address: 2e Weteringplantsoen 21, 1017 ZD Amsterdam

Bankers: Algemene Bank Nederland, Amsterdam No. 54.03.29.924; AMRO Bank, Amsterdam No. 41.13.40.840

Heineken Internationaal Beheer B.V. – Registered Office at Amsterdam – Trade Register Amsterdam No. 103545

JAMES C. WADE III

P.O. Box 103
Montchoisi
1000 Lausanne 19
Switzerland

June 29th, 1992

Hertz Rent-A-Car
Attn. Station Manager
Zurich Airport
8058 Zurich
Switzerland

Dear sir or madam,

On June 24th, I returned a green Ford Fiesta to you which I had
rented for a week. Through some horrible mistake on my part, I
inadvertently left my mother asleep on the back seat! Did you
happen to find her? She is about five feet five, has gray hair,
and answers to the name "Mrs. Wade."

I am a little embarrassed to be writing to you about this, and I hope
that you can understand the predicament that I am in. Please let me
know whether you have found her, or whether another customer
might have accidentally taken her along to some other destination.
If so, maybe next week when I have sorted out a few problems here
in Lausanne I can arrange to pick her up.

Thank you very much in advance for your reply, which I look
forward to receiving as soon as possible.

Yours sincerely,

[signature: James Wade]

JAMES C. WADE III

P.O. Box 103
Montchoisi
1000 Lausanne 19
Switzerland

July 14th, 1992

Hertz Rent-A-Car
Attn. Station Manager
Zurich Airport
8058 Zurich
Switzerland

Dear sir or madam,

On June 29th I wrote enquiring whether my mother had been found
in the rental car I returned on the 24th of that month. Despite the
fact that this is obviously a pressing family matter, I was surprised
that you did not respond to my letter.

I am now quite anxious to find and retrieve her as soon as possible,
as she has a doctor's appointment on July 23rd at 2 in the afternoon,
which she cannot miss. Could you please urgently check once more
and let me know if she has turned up?

I look forward to receiving your answer.

Yours sincerely,

PS. Perhaps the reason you did not reply earlier is that you were
    embarrassed to bring up the subject of my reimbursing you the
    cost of her meals and so on while she was in your safekeeping.
    Please be assured I will pay in full, if you would be so kind as to
    present receipts.

Hertz AG
Headquarters for Switzerland

8952 Schlieren / Zurich
Ifangstrasse 8
Telecopy 01 / 730 12 44
Phone 01 / 732 11 11

Mr.
James C. Wade III
P.O. Box 103
Montchoisi
1000 Lausanne 19

Schlieren, July 27, 1992

<u>Car rental at Zurich Airport</u>

Dear Sir,

Your letter regarding the above car rental has been forwarded to our attention. Upon receipt of the latter, we immediately had this matter thoroughly investigated.

Considering the very particular type of problem exposed, we kindly ask you to please contact the undersigned at the following number:

01 732 12 09

Thank you for your business and for bringing this matter to our attention.

Sincerely,

HERTZ AG

Thomas Huizer
Customer Relations

JAMES C. WADE III

P.O. Box 103
Montchoisi
1000 Lausanne 19
Switzerland

July 30th, 1992

Hertz AG
Attn. Mr. Thomas Huizer,
Customer Relations
Ifangstrasse 8
8952 Schlieren/Zurich
Switzerland

Re: <u>Car rental, misplaced woman (mother)</u>

Dear Mr. Huizer,

Thank you for your letter dated July 27th. I have not been able
to reach you by phone, as you suggested, because of some kind of
technical problem. Each time I call you, I get a recording in
Japanese. There is about two minutes of babble, then a bunch of
"banzai!"s. This seems unusual for a company like Hertz. Are you
sure you gave me the right number?

Anyway, let me bring you up to date on the subject at hand. Dr.
Desmond Ballou, my mother's doctor, says that she did not show up
for her July 23rd appointment. I am getting very concerned, since
she could have been rented two dozen times and driven anywhere in
Europe by now. Could you please put out a Hertz APB and let me
know if she has been spotted?

Thank you again for your near-timely response.

Yours sincerely,

[signature]

PS. Dr. Ballou says that a no-show fee will apply. Will you
     cover this?

Hertz AG
Headquarters for Switzerland

8952 Schlieren / Zurich
Ifangstrasse 8
Telecopy 01 / 730 12 44
Phone 01 / 732 11 11

Mr.
James C. Wade III
P.O. Box 103
Montchoisi
1000 Lausanne 19

Schlieren, August 3, 1992

Car rental at Zurich Airport

Dear Sir,

With regard to your recent letter we regret that you had to take the time to contact us once again.

Please note the phone number quoted in our last letter i.e. 01/732.12.09 is correct and there is no such "Japanese" recording.

Furthermore, although we are always concerned when customers lose personal property in our vehicles, one of the conditions of the rental contract, is that we cannot assume liability for personal property or for any consequence of their loss and this especially when one can not retrieve the rental.

However, being extremely concerned about this matter, we are willing to investigate it further and for this we kindly ask you to provide us with the following information:

1) Rental agreement number or invoice number.
2) Credit card account number with which the rental was paid.
3) Color of the car and model (for information, we usually have no green car in our fleet).
4) Date and place of pick-up.
5) Date and place of return.
6) Your telephone number and times at which you can be reached in case of emergency.
7) The registration of the rented vehicle if known.
8) The exact name of renter should the vehicle not have been rented in your name.

Should the questions number; 2; 3; 4; 6 and 8; not be answered, we will not be in a position to investigate this matter any further and will consider this file as closed. Especially that you will certainly understand that had we found the lost item, we would immediately have contacted the renter quoted on the contract.

We can assure you that we highly appreciate your business.

Sincerely,

H E R T Z   A G

Thomas Huizer
Customer Relations

JAMES C. WADE III

P.O. Box 103
Montchoisi
1000 Lausanne 19
Switzerland

August 6th, 1992

Hertz AG
Attn. Mr. Thomas Huizer, Customer Relations
Ifangstrasse 8
8952 Schlieren/Zurich
Switzerland

Re: Your letter of August 3rd

Dear Mr. Huizer,

Thanks for writing me back. I feel sure we will be able to get to the bottom of this incident soon.

Please note that I was a bit taken aback by your referral to my mother as an "item" or as "personal property." I believe at one time my mother and father *together* could have been considered an "item" but never anyone's property per se. And I am quite certain that my mother would not condone the term "pick-up" in reference to herself (see your question 4).

Notwithstanding this odd language, here is the information you require:

1. I don't know. Unfortunately my doctor shredded all this.
2. Since five years ago I always pay in cash. My Diners Card was taken away from me in 1987 because I tried to use it to finance a corporate takeover.
3. Can't say for sure. I think it was a Ford, with an Italian-sounding name. Fiesta, Carpaccio, Rigatoni, something like that. Color: kind of fungus-colored.
4. We got the car, if that's what you mean, at the airport in Zurich, around the middle of June.
5. June 24th, same exact place.
6. I am at the Jim Morrison Clinic in Lausanne, 24 hours a day. I am not allowed phone calls during rest periods.
7. No idea. I think it had Missouri plates.
8. It was rented in my mother's name, as she did most of the driving till she got tired there at the end. Check either Dame Maria-Theresia Wade-Futtock or Edna St. Vincent Millay.

Looking forward to hearing from you again soon.

Yours,

[signature]

111

JAMES C. WADE III

P.O. Box 103
Montchoisi
1000 Lausanne 19
Switzerland

August 8th, 1992

Hertz AG
Attn. Mr. Thomas Huizer, Customer Relations
Ifangstrasse 8
8952 Schlieren/Zurich
Switzerland

Re: Lost mother

Dear Mr. Huizer,

Hot on the heels of my last letter to you, I thought I would let you
know that my mother has been found!

It turns out she went all the way to Finland in the back seat of an
Avis rent-a-car. (It was red after all. I am sort of color-blind.) She
says she had an interesting trip, and got to know the driver of the
car very well, a longshoreman from Denver who was taking his
first-ever European vacation. She says she plans to visit him this fall
and see if he can get her a job in the docks.

I am terribly sorry about the mix-up and all the trouble you went to!
You've been fairly helpful. Hope to meet you one day. Till then,
best regards from the clinic,

Yours sincerely,

[signature]

W. STUART WADE

3023 N. Clark Street, No. 789
Chicago, Illinois 60657
USA

September 1st, 1992

European Space Agency
Attn. Astronaut Training
Rue Mario-Nikis
F- 75738 Paris Cedex 15
France

Dear sirs,

My next-door neighbor (whose name I cannot give you, as you will appreciate in a moment) is an air force pilot. He mostly flies F-18s. As an unofficial guest on board, my dog Ubaldo has made about twenty supersonic flights, encountering forces up to 6 G's without any serious side effects, except for an apparent 8-10 inch increase in the length of his tongue - would this be normal?

At any rate, since Ubaldo is now experienced in this kind of thing, I would like to sign him up for membership of the crew of a future space shuttle mission. Rather than write directly to NASA, I thought I'd contact you first, because it seems there is always one token European on each shuttle crew, so maybe you have some good advice on how to get Ubaldo on board as the token dog. If not, do you have any other ideas how Ubaldo could get into space?

I hope you see the potential value in taking Ubaldo along. It would present you with numerous opportunities for further experimentation and expanding our horizons of knowledge. He's a good dog. Could you please let me know what you think?

Sincerely yours,

W. Stuart Wade

PS. Ubaldo is certainly house trained. The only accident he's had while flying was very minor, and the pilot was obviously wearing a helmet.

european space agency
agence spatiale européenne

H/CAB/KER/ac/6811   Paris, 22 September 1992

Dear Mr Wade

Thank you for your letter dated September 1. We were interested to learn about Ulbado's experience as an Air Force dog. Our experimentation Committee has decided to consider his application for flight (by the way, is it a he or a she ?) aboard Hermes in 2098. As he is house-trained, we might envisage an earlier mission in the case of another passenger withdrawing.

Up to that date we have a long waiting list which includes an armadillos, a frozen baby plesiosaurus, unicorns, raccoons, vampire bats, a sea horse and his jockey...

With your agreement we could also draft an MOU with the Russians to include the necessary provisions covering Ulbado's mission to MIR, where he could perhaps meet Laïka. If the old lady is still "available", a biological experiment could be conducted which might lead to the first generation of space doggies.

There are however four points of concern. The first one relates to space walks with the dogs. Following the NASA/Italy tethered satellite experiment conducted a few weeks ago, it appears it would be difficult to keep them on a lead. Secondly, astronauts aboard Hermes do not wear helmets permanently. Although Ubaldo is house-trained, we would have to ask a diaper manufacter to sponsor the mission, which then could be named "pampers Missions". Thirdly, the increase in the length of his tongue is a bit of a tongue-twister but this could be overcome by means of a space-qualified muzzle. Finally, reentry is a problem as we would not dare to send you back a hot dog.

In the meantime, if you do not want to wait for Hermes and if it is particularly a flight opportunity with a shuttle mission which interests you, I would suggest to write to NASA.

P.S : If everything fails, would Ubaldo accept an Albedo observation mission ?

Yours sincerely,

K.-E. Reuter
Head of the Director General's Cabinet

8-10 rue Mario-Nikis 75738 Paris Cedex 15 - ℘ (33.1) 42 73 76 54
Télécopieur (33.1) 42 73 75 60 - Télex ESA 202746 - Télégr. Spaceurop Paris

114

european space agency
agence spatiale européenne
european astronauts centre
europäisches astronautenzentrum

Mr. Stuart Wade
3023 North Clark Street 789
Chicago
IL 60657
USA

Köln, 23 September 1992

Your Ref. :

Our Ref. : EAC/CO/WP/uf/92-343

Dear Sir,

Many thanks for your offer which you presumably made on behalf of your dog Ubaldo.

We can, unfortunately, only support candidatures of animals, having the nationality of one of our Member States. As we assume that this is not the case for Ubaldo we have to refer to our international partner, NASA, who might accommodate your request more properly.

We are happy to note that Ubaldo is a good dog but would strongly recommend you to refrain from pursuing additional flights as the increasing length of his tongue might disqualify him in further selection processes. Morever, he might even trip over it.

Wishing you a lot of success with your dog's career.

Yours faithfully,

W. Peeters

P.S. I added some literature on ESA-EAC for Ubaldo.

JAMES C. WADE III

P.O. Box 103
Montchoisi
1000 Lausanne 19
Switzerland

October 28th, 1994

Gösgen Nuclear Power Plant
Attn. Catering Manager
4658 Däniken
Switzerland

Dear sir:

I am organizing a small Christmas party on December 17th of this year and wondered if it would be possible to rent your containment building.

There would be about 15 guests, and we would certainly all be gone before 2 a.m. It goes without saying that we would not fool around with any dials, open any doors, etc.

If this would work out, can you suggest any particular items of clothing we should wear that might glow if they pick up some background radiation? We thought this would make for an especially festive atmosphere.

I look forward to hearing from you soon, so that I can get the invitations printed up.

Yours sincerely,

[signature]

P.S. Is parking possible inside the cooling tower?

November 3th, 1994
94/11856/BAC/cl

Kernkraftwerk **Gösgen**

James C. Wade III
P.O. Box 103
Montchoisi
1000 **Lausanne** 19

Your request: Containment section for a Christmas party

Dear Sir

We acknowledge receipt of your letter, dated October 28,1994, with which you inquire whether it would be possible to rent our containment building for a small Christmas party.

We thank you very much for the interest you take in our power station. Unfortunately, we cannot rent any section of our plant for private events.

However, if you and your family, friends or colleagues wish to visit our plant, we would be very pleased to arrange a guided tour for you. You will find the necessary information annexed in the small visitors' brochure.

Yours faithfully

KERNKRAFTWERK GÖSGEN-DÄNIKEN AG

W. STUART WADE

3023 N. Clark Street, No. 789
Chicago, Illinois 60657

September 1st, 1992

Dewar's Scotch
c/o Schieffelin & Somerset Importers
2 Park Avenue, 17th Floor
New York, New York 10016

Dear sirs,

Your series of "Dewar's Profiles" is one of the truly outstanding ad
campaigns in the history of American advertising. I find them fascinating, and always read the entire ad - more than I can say for
about 99% of the ads out there! How many Profiles have you run
by now? I'll bet it's at least 2,000.

I am writing to recommend my brother James, an avid Dewar's
drinker (most of the time in moderation), as the subject of an
upcoming Profile. I don't know if you accept "nominations from
the floor", so to speak, but if you do, I think you would find James
an excellent subject, thanks to his generally upright character,
unique accomplishments and, since an unfortunate accident three
years ago, his rugged good looks.

I've already taken the liberty of composing a draft Profile of James
for you. Use it with my compliments (I wouldn't dream of asking
for cash), and feel free to make minor changes.

Again, congratulations on this great ad series and for the best
darn Scotch on the market. Please let me know when you expect
this ad to run.

Yours sincerely,

W. Stuart Wade

encl.: Dewar's Profile of James C. Wade III

Dewar's Profiles (pronounced "Do-ers")

Name: James C. Wade III

Home: Lausanne, Switzerland

Age: "As young as you feel," he feels at least 35

Profession: Pastry chef/author/weekend goatherd

Hobby: Cataloging livestock diseases

Accomplishment: Wrote the definitive dessert cookbook
                   I Scream, You Scream, We All Scream from his
                   hospital bed, while recovering from an acci-
                   dent in which he got his head caught in a
                   lawnmower. Book soared to number 71 on
                   the *Kokomo Literary Huzzah* bestseller list.

Last Book Read: Leonard Maltin's *Movie and Video Guide*,
                   cover to cover. "Kept my interest all the way
                   through - that's the sign of a truly good book."

Quote: "Never before in the course of human events
                   have so many owed so much to so few."
                   [Dewar's: You might want to come up with
                   something else here. James is more the strong
                   silent type.]

Profile: Misanthropic, a bit of a loner, cares for people
                   about as much as he likes bacteria. But an
                   excellent consumer of...

Scotch: Dewar's "White Label" with water. "Goats be
                   damned."

September 14, 1992

Mr. W. Stuart Wade
3023 North Clark Street
Chicago, IL 60657

Dear Mr. Wade,

Thank you for the submission of James Wade as a candidate for the Dewar's Profile advertising campaign. Since 1969, nearly 100 individuals have been part of this well-known campaign, which has helped Dewar's "White Label" become the number one Scotch in the United States.

From time to time, we review these requests, but we generally produce only 3-4 Dewar's Profiles each year. So although it may be a while before you hear from us again, be assured that we will keep Jame's materials in our files, and will contact you should we need more information.

In the meantime, we hope you continue to enjoy Dewar's "White Label" fine Scotch Whisky.

Sincerely,

LEO BURNETT U.S.A.

Laura Zeeman
Assistant Account Executive
Dewar's "White Label"

LZ/ew

JAMES C. WADE III

c/o Shack World
P.O. Box 103
Montchoisi
1000 Lausanne 19
Switzerland

May 23rd, 1992

American Business Lists, Inc.
P.O. Box 27347
Omaha, Nebraska 68127
USA

Dear sirs,

Can you help me assemble a mailing list of all the businesses in the
Kansas-Nebraska-Iowa "golden triangle" whose names contain
the words WORLD, HUT, or SHACK?

These companies form the target group for the services of my
consulting firm, Shack World. We assist these companies with
marketing projects, advertising, etc. It has been our experience that
most companies with names like The Burger Hut have precious little marketing imagination and really could use the help.

In addition, I have just founded a sister company called The Hut
Shack which provides accounting and tax advice. Our client list
includes Hammer World, a chain of hardware stores; The Bean Hut,
a Mexican diner; and Skin Shack, a video rental emporium.

I look forward to hearing from you soon.

Yours sincerely,

[signature]

PS. In really dire cases, you will find the word SHACK spelled
     SHAK. These companies are usually desperate. I would also
     like a list of these firms, preferably on a separate printout, as
     they may be interested in my customized computer program
     SHAKWARE.

121

• 5711 SOUTH 86TH CIRCLE • P.O. BOX 27347 • OMAHA, NEBRASKA 68127 •
EXECUTIVE OFFICE: 402/593-4500 • SALES: 402/331-7169 FAX: 402/331-1505

August 21, 1992

Mr. James C. Wade III
c/o Shack World
P.O. Box 103
Montchoisi
1000 Lausanne 19
SWITZERLAND

Dear James:

I apologize for the time in which it has taken American
Business List to respond.

At present we have approximately 40,075 records with WORLD,
HUT, or SHACK in their title. The estimated cost of this
list would be $4500.00 plus shipping. It will take us
approximately two days to process this order. Shipping
would take approximately 10 working days.

Method of payment for this order is company check or credit
card.

I look forward to hearing from you.

Sincerely,

Joel E. Cornman

JC/kb

122

JAMES C. WADE III

c/o Shack World
P.O. Box 103
Montchoisi
1000 Lausanne 19
Switzerland

August 31st, 1992

American Business Information, Inc.
Attn. Mr. Joel E. Cornman
P.O. Box 27347
Omaha, Nebraska 68127
USA

Dear Mr. Cornman,

Thank you for your letter of August 21st. I was flabbergasted that your computer found over 40,000 firms whose names contain the words WORLD, SHACK, or HUT. What a gold mine for my business! However, I can't help thinking there must be a mistake somewhere. May I ask a few more questions so we can pinpoint whether an error might have cropped up?

1. Are you sure that you confined your search to the Nebraska-Iowa-Kansas "Bermuda Triangle"? I didn't think there could even be that many businesses in all three states TOTAL. In fact I was under the impression that there were only about 150 businesses of any kind in the entire state of Iowa, unless you count hog farms.

2. Did you by any chance count all the Pizza Huts as separate businesses? This would vastly inflate the final count. Shack World would only deal with Pizza Hut at the H.Q. level so it should only be on the list once (if it's in Nebraska, Iowa, or Kansas, that is).

3. Is it possible that your computer program somehow also found businesses whose names contain the letters W-O-R-L-D, S-H-A-C-K, or H-U-T, but which are not legitimately in our target group, such as the Worldwide Fund for Nature, or E. F. Hutton?

Once these issues are cleared up, I will be in a better position to determine the value of your list. One last question: Do you accept Shell credit cards?

Looking forward to your reply.

Yours sincerely,

[signature]

· 5711 SOUTH 86TH CIRCLE · P.O. BOX 27347 · OMAHA, NEBRASKA 68127 ·
EXECUTIVE OFFICE: 402/593-4500 · SALES: 402/331-7169 FAX: 402/331-1505

October 6, 1992

Mr. James C. Wade III
SHACK WORLD
P.O. Box 103
MONTCHOISI
1000 LAUSANNE 19
SWITZERLAND

RE: Your letter of August 31st

Dear Mr. Wade:

Thank you for your letter. You are correct, the 40,000 records I
quoted you August 21st were for the total United States.

At present there are 311,115 businesses in Iowa, Nebraska and
Kansas (125,108 in Iowa), in that area there are 1190 with the word
World, Shack, or Hut in their name. All Pizza Huts are included in
this list, but it would be possible to select only headquarters.
Worldwide and E.F. Hutton would not appear on this list.

The estimated cost of this list would be $850.00 plus shipping. We
can accept either MasterCard, Visa, American Express, or a company
check drawn on a U.S. Bank.

Sincerely,

Joel E. Cornman

JC/kb

124

JAMES C. WADE III

c/o Shack World
P.O. Box 103
Montchoisi
1000 Lausanne 19
Switzerland

November 4th, 1992

American Business Information, Inc.
Attn. Mr. Joel E. Cornman
P.O. Box 27347
Omaha, Nebraska 68127
USA

Re: WORLD / SHACK / HUT businesses

Dear Mr. Cornman,

Many thanks for your letter dated October 6th. Apologies for the delay in my reply; I seem to have come down with a touch of brucellosis.

I am glad that you were able to clear up the slight discrepancy between the 40,000+ business names from throughout the US of A and the 1,190 that exist in our NE-KS-IA target market. For a moment there I thought we had hit pay dirt.

However, I'm afraid that we will not be going ahead with the project just now. We have become involved in some litigation with a heavy metal rock band over the use of our slogan "Let's Shack Up". Our lawyers advise that we postpone any marketing campaigns using this motto pending a court decision, which is expected in about five years.

Thank you very much for your assistance up to this point. I look forward to getting in touch with you again then.

Sincerely yours,

[signature]

125

W. STUART WADE

3023 N. Clark Street, No. 789
Chicago, Illinois 60657

July 20th, 1992

TWA Frequent Flyer Bonus Program
P.O. Box 800
Fairview Village, Pennsylvania 19409

Dear sirs,

I would like to register my dog as a member of the TWA Frequent
Flyer Bonus Program. As Alejandro has criss-crossed the country
many times on TWA, it only seems fair that he should be accorded
membership privileges. Besides, he could use the bonus miles to
visit his father Dante in Virginia before it is too late.

For your files:

Name:	Alejandro
Address:	As above
Age:	6 (or 42 if you prefer)
Breed:	Mixed
Meals:	Reduced-calorie preferred

Thank you very much in advance.

Sincerely yours,

W. Stuart Wade

0148070D

TWA
FREQUENT FLIGHT BONUS PROGRAM

**Here is your FFB® mileage balance and
recent program information.** Remember, your
FFB miles have no expiration date, and will always
be available to you. (Be sure to read important
FFB Program information on the reverse side.)

FFB account: **99418340**

Mileage balance: **0**

As of: **9/10/92**

ALEJANDRO WADE, CANINE
C/O W. STUART WADE
3023 N CLARK ST
CHICAGO   IL 60657-5200

TWA PROUDLY ANNOUNCES NEW NONSTOP SERVICE BETWEEN ATLANTA AND HOUSTON
-AND- BETWEEN ATLANTA AND BOSTON, EFFECTIVE OCTOBER 25, 1992.

JAMES C. WADE III

P.O. Box 103
Montchoisi
1000 Lausanne 19
Switzerland

May 13th, 1992

<u>Penthouse</u> Magazine
Attn: Editor, Letters Department
1965 Broadway
New York, New York 10023-5965
USA

Dear Sir,

For many years (since puberty, in fact), I have been an avid reader of <u>Penthouse</u> letters. Often these letters seem so outlandish that I think they must be invented, but looking back over my own life, I must admit that I too have had my fair share of experiences that your readers might find piquant and/or revolting.

My favorite in this category is one I would like to write up for publication. However, I am a little concerned about the possibility of legal trouble, as the other people involved are both rather well-known in their respective circles and might not want my story to be publicized.

The woman is the wife of a United States Senator, and the man is a flamboyant network anchorman, known throughout the country. It is hard to see how I can disguise their identities. Therefore, before I write up my eyewitness account of their six days and six nights at the Indianapolis Hyatt Regency in all its astounding detail, can you suggest how I should change the details that unmistakably point to the two of them? Do you think I should omit the fact that "Mrs Jones" has flaming red hair and only one leg, even though a good deal of the action revolves around this point? Just as important, how should I camouflage "Mr Smith"? Would it be enough to say he works for a different network, or should I change his profession to something else entirely, like running a factory that makes high-grade dog food?

Once these details are worked out, I'm very sure that you (and <u>Penthouse</u> readers everywhere) will appreciate this story, which for me was the absolute highlight of 1989. I look forward to hearing from you.

Yours sincerely,

[signature]

GENERAL MEDIA PUBLISHING GROUP, 1965 BROADWAY, NEW YORK, NY 10023-5965. 212-496-6100. FAX 212-580-3693

June 29, 1992

James C. Wade III
P.O. Box 103
Montchoisi
1000 Lausanne 19
Switzerland

Dear Mr. Wade:

Thank you for your recent letter.

May I suggest that if you're interested in submitting a piece to "Forum" that you change all the necessary details as to not make the people knowable. Make the gentlemen just an executive at anytype of company. And changed the names and necessary physical details of the people involved. If you keep in mind that the shorter the piece is the more likely it is to be published that should help you a great deal.

I've enclosed the guildeline for PENTHOUSE, and our other "special publications" which should help some also.

Thank you.

Sincerely,

Lavada Blanton
Associate Editor
Editor, "Forum" column

PENTHOUSE

JAMES C. WADE III

P.O. Box 103
Montchoisi
1000 Lausanne 19
Switzerland

July 3rd, 1992

<u>Penthouse</u> Magazine
Attn. Ms. Lavada Blanton, Associate Editor
1965 Broadway
New York, New York 10023-5965
USA

Dear Ms. Blanton,

Thank you very much for your letter of June 29th which was a great help to me.

However, you mentioned that a guideline for Penthouse letters was enclosed, although the envelope did not contain one. I wonder if I could trouble you to send me a copy to keep by my gun hand, as it were. (Also for your other "special publications" - the mind boggles!) I am sure that with this professional help, I will be able to write up my experience so that the central characters are not recognizable, despite their sordid uniqueness.

Also, thanks for the tip about keeping it short. I will try to be as succinct as I can without sacrificing any of the lurid detail necessary to the plot.

Looking forward to hearing from you again,

Yours sincerely,

[signature]

PS. In case you have run out of written guidelines, all I really need to know is whether it is all right to mention power tools by their brand names? Maybe you could just drop me a line that says "yes" or "no." Thanks!

GENERAL MEDIA PUBLISHING GROUP, 1965 BROADWAY, NEW YORK, NY 10023-5965. 212-496-6100. FAX 212-580-3693

July 30, 1992

James C. Wade III
P.O. Box 103
Montchoisi
1000 Lausanne 19
Switzerland

Dear Mr. Wade:

Why do I have this feeling that I'm not going to be getting a letter lenght
piece from you, but rather an intricately laid out long story.

Please don't mention brand names, just keep the entire thing as generic as
possible.   I made sure to include the guidelines this go around.

Thanks!

Sincerely,

Lavada Blanton
Associate Editor
Editor, "Forum"

PENTHOUSE

W. STUART WADE

3023 N. Clark Street, No. 789
Chicago, Illinois 60657
USA

August 14th, 1992

Cartier Limited
175 New Bond Street
London W1Y 0QA
England

Dear sirs,

I have been an admirer of your beautiful jewelry for many years.
My grandmother owned a wonderful Edwardian piece which she
bought from you in the 1930's, containing a large emerald in the
shape of an amethyst. As I recall, it was quite stunning.

My brother James and I are both jewelry designers now, and we
believe we have come up with a concept Cartier would find very
interesting. In actual fact, our jewelry is not designed to be worn
by women but by cows, horses, and other large domestic animals.
Visually, these items are among the most striking and unusual to
come along in the 20th century. The bovine teat rings alone are so
beautiful and ornate that we have had requests from dairy farmers
all over Europe and America for custom-made pieces.

An interview with James is being taped at BBC studios in London
during the week of September 14th. As he will already be in
England, he would be happy to spend a full day with you, together
with Mr Samuel Langhorne Kowalski, our animal handler, and a
"model" who is already fitted with some exquisite pieces, including
a tiara which I think you will find absolutely breathtaking. Mr
Kowalski can show your staff how to measure various animals for
rings, bangles, necklaces, etc. - also how to use the special ear-pierc-
ing equipment, as this can sometimes be a bit dodgy.

Could you please drop me a note to suggest a convenient date for
the appointment?

Yours sincerely,

W. Stuart Wade

PS. Do you have a freight elevator capable of accommodating a
small swine?

BY APPOINTMENT
TO H.M. QUEEN ELIZABETH
THE QUEEN MOTHER
JEWELLERS AND GOLDSMITHS

Cartier Ltd

CARTIER S.A. _ 13 RUE DE I A PAIX
PARIS

CARTIER INC _ 653 FIFTH AVENUE
NEW YORK

REGISTERED OFFICE
175-176 NEW BOND STREET
LONDON WIY OQA

REGISTERED IN ENGLAND No. 157267
REGISTERED FOR VAT No. 238-5603-54

TELEPHONE 071-493 6962
TELEX 264441
FAX 071-355 3011

20th August 1992

W. Stuart Wade,
3023 North Clark Street,
Box 789,
Chicago
IL 60657

Dear Sir/Madam,

Thank you for your letter of 14th August. It is nice to hear from an admirer of our fine products.

We look forward to seeing the interview with your brother James on television but doubt that he will be allowed to exhibit the jewellery you talk about as we have strict censorship rules for full frontal presentation. But perhaps if the models were to wear semi transparent lingerie it might pass the censors.

As regards an appointment to view these products in fitting surroundings, we are speaking to a tittled landowner who we hope might rent us suitable pastures.

You mention cows, but do you have jewellery for bulls? If so, I am sure that we could find the ideal venue in the China department of one of England's largest departmental stores.

Yours faithfully

T.M.J. Davidson

PS We regret that our elevators are only designed to accommodate haggis (female variety)

P.O. Box 103
Montchoisi
1000 Lausanne 19, Switzerland

July 13th, 1993

Explorer Shipping Co.
Attn. Lt. Rupert Woodard, Royal Navy (ret.)
1520 Kensington Road
Oak Brook, Illinois 60521, USA

Lieutenant:

By chance I met an old friend from the clinic who mentioned that your company is on the lookout for speakers to give scientific lectures aboard your expedition cruise ships. Look no further! With advanced degrees in paleontology, sociobotany and English Lit., and a keen interest in woodworking, I have done a considerable amount of shipboard lecturing in the past ten years, and thought you might be interested. I've even developed a bit of a following, who may well come along for the ride.

My last stint was aboard the *M/S Spirit of Krasnoyarsk Autonomous Region*, a Russian liquid propane tanker. She took the occasional group of American tree-huggers to some tundra-bedecked rock in the middle of nowhere and left them there for a week while she delivered her cargo. For two years, I gave lectures about the so-called "delicate balance of nature". All was well until the *"Krasny"* went down in an ice storm off Hammerfest, leaving me stranded on Spitzbergen with 34 members of the Northern California chapter of Friends of the Musk Ox. God, those chaps were boring!

Maritime disaster notwithstanding, these little talks of mine were always a resounding success. May I propose the following lectures from my repertoire (all accompanied by slides, of course):

Natural Sciences:
Our Cousins the Lemurs and Marmosets
The Grenade and its Use in
   Big Game Hunting
Naming your Dog
A Cornucopia of Small Animal Burrows

Expedition Advice:
Common Head Injuries
Improvising Dinner:
   10 Delicious Walrus Recipes
Winning Big at Five Card Stud
Choosing the Right
   Corrective Shoes

As my lecture career with the Russians is temporarily on hold, I am available immediately. How is the heating on your ship? (On the *"Krasny"* it got mighty tiresome wearing a parka 24 hours a day.) Shall we try and work something out? I look forward to hearing from you.

Sincerely yours,

[signature]

JAMES C. WADE III

P.O. Box 103
Montchoisi
1000 Lausanne 19
Switzerland

August 30th, 1993

Lt. Rupert Woodard, RN
Explorer Shipping Co.
1520 Kensington Road
Oak Brook, Illinois 60521
USA

Dear Lieutenant:

About six weeks ago - on July 13th to be precise - I fired off a letter to gauge your interest in using me as a shipboard lecturer. To my utter surprise, I've received no reply to date. Have you been away?

In the meantime, you'll be pleased to hear that I've made plans to come see you in Oak Brook and discuss this whole matter face to face. I'll be there the entire week of September 20th, and thought I would pop in and spend Tuesday and Wednesday with you.

As you'll no doubt want to see me do my stuff, I'll be bringing along a set of my lecture slides and wonder if I might trouble you to arrange for a projector and screen for those two days. You won't want to sit through all of the slides, of course, but I was thinking that a representative selection of 2,000 or so ought to give you a fairly good idea of how handy I am with my trusty 35 mm SLR.

The first half of the collection would be foliage - if pressed for time, I'm sure we could skip over some of that. However, I've done quite a bit of auk-and-puffin work, and I'll definitely be bringing those slides, as this is perhaps my very best photography. There's one sequence (400 frames in all) which I used aboard the *"Krasny"* as the basis for a fascinating eight-hour seminar on nest-building.

I can't tell you how much I'm looking forward to working with you. One last thing - can you recommend a decent hotel near your offices? I will need one with special facilities for my dog, who lost his legs in a gardening accident.

Many thanks! See you on the 21st,

Sincerely yours,

TO: JAMES C. WADE 111
        PO BOX 103
        1000 LAUSANNE 19
        SWITZERLAND   7 September 1993

Dear James,

Many thanks for your kind letter of 30 August. I am horrified
to hear that you were awaiting a response to a previous letter, but
have to admit that I did not actually receive it. I would be most
grateful if you could resend it, in order that I may learn a little
more about your backgound.

Your presentation sounds excellent: Unfortunately I will not
be here during the week of 20 September, but our new president,
Peter Reynolds, would be more than happy to hear you out. The nest
building sequence sounds fascinating, and I am very sad to think I
will miss it.

We will book you in at the Oak Brook hills hotel for the week
of 20 September; fortunately they have all the facilities you will
need including a dog rolling service.

I hope you have a safe trip to the US.

Best wishes.

RUPERT WOODARD
DIRECTOR OF OPERATIONS

EXPLORER SHIPPING CORPORATION

1520 Kensington Road Oak Brook, Illinois 60521
Fax: 708.954.2814
Phone: 708.954.2944

135

P.O. Box 103
Montchoisi
1000 Lausanne 19
Switzerland

September 11th, 1993

Lt. Rupert Woodard, RN
Director of Operations,
Explorer Shipping Corp.
1520 Kensington Road
Oak Brook, Illinois 60521
USA

Dear Lt. Woodard,

Thank you for your letter of September 7th. How odd that you never got my first letter - check with your secretary, maybe she shredded it by mistake. Herewith a certified copy.

It is very kind of you to offer to put me up at the Oak Brook Hills Hotel. I assume your offer goes for my wife and children, plus my brother and his family? Altogether I think four rooms would about do it. Are you splurging for meals, too? Many thanks.

Now for the bad news. I'm afraid the trip is going to have to be postponed for a short while, owing to unforeseen financial difficulties. American Express is being a nuisance because I just purchased a house in Florida and charged it to my card. It seems this was over my limit. I expect they may take a month or so to straighten out.

Since you were unavailable to meet me this month anyway, perhaps this works out for the best after all. I appreciate your offering to have the president entertain me, but I really think this seems rather pointless. What does the president of a company really understand about the way things run, anyway? I would much prefer to talk directly with the Man in the Know any day. How does your calender look at the end of October? Drop me a line and let's reschedule. I assume the hotel arrangements stand?

Yours,

[signature]

PS. Would you have any interest in screening a series of slides called "Beat the Experts at Soil Identification"? With commentary, jokes, etc. it runs to just under five hours.

TO: James C. Wade III
      PO BOX 103
      Montchoisi
      1000 Lausanne 19
      Switzerland   1 October 1993

Dear James,

    Many thanks for your letter of 11 September, along with the
certified copy of the original. My sincere apologies for my late
response, but I have been travelling.

    I am extremely sad you were unable to visit us, and that you
have been having trouble with American Express; You must have
bought a big house!

    I will be at the office between 13 and 20 October should you
be able to visit then; I understand your reservations about meeting
with the president! If you let me know In can make the same
reservations at the hotel.(How is your dog by the way?)

    I hope we can work something out; "Beat the experts at soil
identification" sounds really fun, and I know our passengers would
enjoy it. They often ask for "Real earthy expeditions". Does your
brother lecture as well. It would look good if we could advertise
the "Wade Brothers".

    I look forward to hearing from you again soon.

    Best Wishes.

        Rupert Woodard

EXPLORER SHIPPING CORPORATION
———————————
1520 Kensington Road Oak Brook, Illinois 60521
Fax: 708.954.2814
Phone: 708.954.2944

W. STUART WADE

3023 N. Clark Street, No. 789
Chicago, Illinois 60657

October 25th, 1993

Lt. Rupert Woodard, Royal Navy (ret.)
Director of Operations,
Explorer Shipping Corp.
1520 Kensington Road
Oak Brook, Illinois 60521

Dear Lt. Woodard,

My brother James sent me a copy of your letter to him dated October 1st, along with a note suggesting I contact you with some ideas for shipboard lectures we could do together.

I must assume this is another of my brother's rather sad "episodes", and I apologize if you have been inconvenienced by it. The unfortunate truth is that ever since his dog Gunther was injured slightly with some electric hedge clippers last year, James has not been well. He isn't "ill" in the usual sense of the word - rather, as time goes on, he has become obsessed with the notion of travel to exotic places. Perhaps it could be his own emotional need to escape from his memories of himself and Gunther in happier times. Just a guess.

Our sister has uncovered various schemes he has cooked up over the past several months to obtain free plane tickets, cruises, hotel accommodations, and so on from unwary organizations like yours. Sometimes he's been remarkably successful. A few weeks ago she was visiting his apartment and found a first-class airline ticket to Hawaii and a crate containing several thousand dollars' worth of brand-new scuba equipment, plus a certified check for spending money - all compliments of the Vatican.

Once again, please forgive us for any trouble James's letter may have caused.

Sincerely yours,

W. Stuart Wade

PS. What would you think about a lecture series on nematode classification techniques? We could probably put something together for you with a few days' notice.

JAMES C. WADE III

P.O. Box 103
Montchoisi
1000 Lausanne 19
Switzerland

August 17th, 1992

London Weekend Television
Attn. Features Programming Director
Kent House, Upper Ground
London SE1 9LT, England

Dear sir,

Would you have any interest in a weekly documentary series called "The Wade Brothers at Large"? The series, to be narrated by Leonard Nimoy, will follow many of the dangerous, stupid, reckless, and irresponsible exploits my brother Stuart and I have had, or plan to have, all around the world.

The first in the regular series, entitled "The Wade Brothers at the Headwaters of the Amazon," finds us paddling bark canoes upriver for ten weeks, day and night and day, fighting off various tropical illnesses, finally planting the Wade family banner, a sloth rampant with arms akimbo, at the Andean trickle where it all begins. It is gruelling, emotionally draining stuff, a hundred times better than anything Cousteau and his boatload of Frenchmen have ever done.

Other episodes in the hopper:

+ "The Wade Brothers at the Bottom of the World"
+ "Alone with the Wade Brothers on the Serengeti Plain"
+ "The Wade Brothers Take Manhattan"
+ "If the Wade Brothers Ruled the World"
+ "The Wade Brothers Go for Gold"

This last one is my personal favorite. It documents our long struggle with the International Olympic Committee to enter the Biathlon as a team. In some remarkable footage of a particularly long and tiresome set of negotiations, you can actually see Avery Brundage punching Stuart in the stomach.

These 60-minute programs will thrill viewers with the very notion that two simple Americans can change the face of the world, or vice versa. Please confirm that we should begin shooting the exciting pilot episode, "The Wade Brothers Rob Ft. Knox."

Thank you in advance for your interest and support. I look forward to hearing from you.

Yours sincerely,

[signature]

139

LONDON WEEKEND TELEVISION LIMITED
THE LONDON TELEVISION CENTRE UPPER GROUND LONDON SE1 9LT
TELEPHONE: 071-620 1620

DIRECT LINE: DIRECT FAX:

25 August 1992

James C Wade
PO Box 103
Montchoisi
1000 Lausanne 19
Switzerland

Dear James C Wade

Thank you for your recent letter and proposal for a series of
The Wade Brothers at Large?.

I am sorry to say that, at present, we are not in a position to
take this, but thank you for thinking of us here at LWT and may
I wish you the best of luck with your proposal elsewhere.

Yours sincerely

Robin Paxton

Robin Paxton
Controller
Features & Current Affairs

THE QUEEN'S AWARD FOR
EXPORT ACHIEVEMENT

3023 N. Clark Street, No. 789
Chicago, Illinois 60657
USA

August 8th, 1992

Saab Automobile Company AB
Attn. New Product Development
S - 461 80 Trollhättan
Sweden

Dear sirs,

As a long-time (and very satisfied) Saab driver, may I pass
along an idea to you for a product innovation which might make
driving as we now know it obsolete?

The idea: voice-activated standard transmission. Essentially,
you would have to install a small on-board computer which would
shift the car into third gear (for example) whenever the driver
says "third." Of course the computer would have to be sensitive
enough to recognize what the driver is saying, and I imagine he
or she would also have to speak pretty clearly, but this sort of
thing is certainly feasible these days.

As an entreprencur myself - my company manufactures cranial
stereos whose miniaturized speakers are surgically implanted - I
am keenly aware of the need for sharing creative ideas; hence my
letter.

I would like to hear your thoughts on this.

Sincerely yours,

W. Smart Wade

PS. There could be some disadvantages, I suppose. For example, it
would be inadvisable to discuss baseball while driving, but that
is a small sacrifice for the convenience gained.

 **SAAB**

Telefax	Date	Our reference
78474	1992–11–18	TDE–BR–N418
Direct dialling No	Your date	Your reference

Handled by

Nils–Gunnar Svensson TDEF A4–1   85428

Mr. W. Stuart Wade
3023 North Clark Street
Box 789
Chicago, IL, 60 657
USA

Copies: T(TX–658),TD,TDE,
TDEF.

Concerning new product development

Dear Mr. Wade,

In reply to your letter of Aug, 8, 1992, we would like to give you the following information.

Our long- and short term development plans are today very solid, and are totally focused on the goal to meet the up-coming emission- and fuel economy requirements worldwide, with a specific effort for California.

To reach this goal, all experience from our current fleet of engines and transmission units must form the base for further development. This development work is now running, leaving no extra capacity for design or development work for projects outside our own schedule.

Based on this, we have to, accordingly, decline your offer for alternate transmission systems.

Yours cincerely,

Saab Automobile AB
Product Development
Drive Train
Concept Studies/Fuels and Lubricants

Nils-Gunnar Svensson

Postal address	Telephone	Teletex	Telex	Bank giro account	Postal giro account
Saab Automobile AB					
S-461 80 Trollhättan	Nat. 0520 - 850 00				
Sweden	Int. +46 520 850 00	8285049 SAABTH	42110 saabth s	551-7586	13 65 99-8
IN 9901438 (33/07) 90-03					

JAMES C. WADE III

P.O. Box 103
Montchoisi
1000 Lausanne 19
Switzerland

August 30th, 1993

Kruger National Park
Skukuza 1350
Republic of South Africa

Attn. Sales Dept.

Dear sirs,

I have heard from many visitors to your country that the world's
finest animal preserves are to be found in South Africa.

As a man who is not willing to settle for anything but the very best, I
would like to stock up on these preserves so that I will always have
some on hand to serve my guests and family. May I please order
twelve jars to be delivered to me at the above address?

Just let me know how you would like me to pay for them. Many
thanks in advance. I am looking forward to tasting your delightful
canned products.

Yours sincerely,

[signature]

Nasionale Krugerwildtuin
Privaatsak X402, Skukuza, 1350
Tel: (01311) 65611
Faks (01311) 65611 x 2219

Kruger National Park
Private Bag X402, Skukuza, 1350
Tel: (01311) 65611
Fax (01311) 65611 x 2219

IK.30/1
PDP\enqwade.let

20 October 1993

Mr James C. Wade III
P O Box 103
Montchoisi
1000 LAUSANNE 19
SWITZERLAND

Dear Mr Wade

Thank you for your letter dated 30 August 1993.

The product to which you refer is the canned meat of animals, usually buffalo, which in the interests of conservation and field management, have had to be culled. Due to the lengthy drought we have experienced here in the Kruger National Park, natural attrition has reduced our buffalo population to the point where culling is not desirable. I regret, therefore, to advise you that we unable to comply with your request.

Yours sincerely

P S DU PLESSIS
GENERAL MANAGER: VISITOR SERVICES
for EXECUTIVE DIRECTOR, KNP

sdr/PDP

ALLE KORRESPONDENSIE MOET AAN DIE UITVOERENDE DIREKTEUR GERIG WORD   ALL CORRESPONDENCE TO BE ADDRESSED TO THE EXECUTIVE DIRECTOR

| Nasionale Parke: | Kruger | Kalahari | Addo | Bergkwagga | Bontebok | Golden Gate | Tsitsikamma | Zuurberg | Richtersveld |
| National Parks: | Augrabies | Karoo | Weskus | Vaalbos | Tankwa | Wildernis | Knysna | Kransberg | |

144

W. STUART WADE

3023 North Clark Street, No. 789
Chicago, Illinois 60657
USA

August 4th, 1992

Christ Water Softeners
Hauptstrasse 192
4047 Aesch
Switzerland

Dear sirs,

I am studying for the priesthood at the St. Larry's Academy of the
Loop here in Chicago. I am majoring in theology with a minor in
marketing and advertising, and hope to combine all these disci-
plines in order to attract more parishioners into the church. Our
market share, as you may know, has been slipping in recent years,
and I hope to help reverse the trend.

On a recent trip to Switzerland, I happened to notice one of your
water purifiers in the American consulate, and an interesting idea
occurred to me which I'd like to develop with you. It could help
not only the Catholic church, but your export sales as well.

I would like to explore with you the possibility of installing state-
of-the-art "Christ" brand water purifiers in Catholic churches
throughout Chicagoland (eventually all of North America), replacing the present baptismal fonts and holy water stoups, which are
mostly made of marble and, in my opinion, only reinforce the old-
fashioned image of the church.

Your brand name, Christ, is of course well-known in the church,
and I feel you should capitalize on this awareness. Seeing "Christ"
in those bold red letters on the side of the new baptismal font,
parishioners could only feel pride and confidence that they were
getting the real McCoy.

Could you please have your export manager write me at the above
address to let me know whether you would like to develop this idea,
or if perhaps you are already working with the Church in any other
countries. I haven't yet asked my bishop about the idea, as I would
like to spring it on him as a surprise, if you'll pardon the pun.

Thank you, and may God bless,

W. Stuart Wade

W. STUART WADE

3023 N. Clark Street, No. 789
Chicago, Illinois 60657
USA

November 2nd, 1992

Christ Water Softeners
Hauptstrasse 192
4047 Aesch
Switzerland

Dear sirs,

On August 4th of this year, I sent you the enclosed letter, but I fear
you may have not received it, as I have not heard anything from
you in all this time.

I am still a Believer in this project, and would like to point out one
additional reason why I think it could be a business success.
Besides the religious reasons mentioned in my last letter, using
your products would be much more hygienic: dirty fingers in the
holy water are a well-known vector of contagious diseases,
accounting for over 1500 cases of swine flu among Catholics in
Illinois every year, to cite but one well-documented example.

Meanwhile, I have broken the news to my bishop, who is jumping
up and down for it. Please let us know whether we can count on
your cooperation.

Sincerely,

W. Stuart Wade

CHRIST
WATER · AIR DIVISION

Mr. W. Stuart Wade
3023 North Clark Street
Box 789
Chicago, IL 60657
USA

November 12, 1992   VN/SP

Dear Mr. Wade:

We apologize for not having answered earlier.

Your proposal sounds interesting from a marketing point-of-view. Unfortunately, Christ has no US representatives nor local organizations servicing or products. However, a local service support would be essential before developing your idea.

Thank you for your letter.

Very truly yours
C H R I S T L T D

Dr. V. Nestler

W. STUART WADE

3023 N. Clark Street, No. 789
Chicago, Illinois 60657

May 12th, 1992

Word Ways Magazine
Attn. Purchasing Dept.
Spring Valley Road
Morristown, New Jersey 07960

Dear sir or madam (I'm Adam),

I have found palindromes fascinating and amusing ever since I was a young boy and was first shown the one about "a man, a plan, a canal, Panama!" by my fourth grade teacher Mrs Bollob.

In 1987, tired of merely jotting down palindromes invented by other people, I began to compose some myself. I would like to know if your magazine can make use of any. Here are two of my best so far:

1. He knows a fat man called Ella Cnamtafaswonkeh.

2. I got hang of fog, nah, Togi!

In the case of No. 1 above, of course I'm aware that a man, strictly speaking, is unlikely to be named "Ella." Nevertheless, just by adding a common Zulu surname (look in any Natal telephone directory), you have a splendid 37-letter palindrome.

As for No. 2, "Togi" was the actual name of a neighbor's feisty little Rutburg terrier. One day, in an exceptionally heavy fog, he was run over by a van delivering linoleum tiles. So this one has some historical grounding in fact.

Please let me know whether you would be interested in purchasing these or any other palindromes at the rock-bottom price of $30 a pair. Many thanks in advance for your reply. I look forward very much to hearing from you with your order.

Yours sincerely,

W. Stuart Wade

Spring Valley Road
Morristown, New Jersey 07960
June 3 1992

Dear Mr. Wade,

I am afraid that I have no interest in purchasing palindromes at $30 the pair (or any other price). Most constructors are in the game for pleasure rather than profit, and the glory of seeing their palindrome in print is reward enough. Word Ways is a scholarly journal rather than a mass-circulation magazine, and does not pay its contributors for their material. If we did, we could not afford to publish.

Your first palindrome is an example of a "Cheater's Palindrome", explored in Word Ways to some extent about a year and a half ago("Baha? Peka? Orca-a-a-a!" croaked Ahab; a phoney: yenohpa!).

Sincerely,

A. Ross Eckler

W. STUART WADE

3023 N. Clark Street, No. 789
Chicago, Illinois 60657

December 3rd, 1992

Boy Scouts of America
Attn. Mr. Ben Love, Chief Scout
1325 Walnut Hill Lane
Irving, Texas 75015

Dear Chief Love:

As a boy growing up in Australia, I was quite active in scouting and
attained the rank of Wombat Scout in a near-record 12 1/2 years.

I mention this to show how seriously I have always taken the
Movement and, with it, the Boy Scout Oath itself, which I still
remember reciting every morning on the banks of the Gottawong
Gully, even in violent hailstorms.

Have you given any thought to bringing the Oath more up to date?
The original adjectives are certainly qualities worth striving for
("trustworthy, brave, loyal," etc.), but they pale a bit next to the
demands of the 1990's, don't you think? If you agree, I'd like to
submit, via your office, the following adjectives for consideration
by a Special Oath Adjective Committee (SOAK) at the next
Jamboree:

> Aware, Laid-Back, Caring,
> Bodacious, Sensitive, Hetero,
> and Politically Correct.

I would also like to propose a new merit badge in Self-Actualization.
The badge itself could be a large green "M" for "Maslow."

I look forward to receiving your endorsement. Many thanks for
your support, and keep up the excellent work,

Sincerely yours,

W. Stuart Wade

BOY SCOUTS OF AMERICA

National Office
1325 West Walnut Hill Lane
P.O. Box 152079, Irving, Texas 75015-2079
214-580-2000

Ben H. Love
Chief Scout Executive

December 8, 1992

Mr. W. Stuart Wade
3023 N. Clark Street #789
Chicago, IL 60657

Dear Mr. Wade:

The Scout Oath has served well since the inception of the Boy Scouts of America. There are no plans underway to revise the oath in any way.

Your suggestion is appreciated.

Sincerely,

Ben H. Love
Chief Scout Executive

jk

151

W. STUART WADE

3023 N. Clark Street, No. 789
Chicago, Illinois 60657

January 10th, 1993

The Carpet People
1421 W. Devon Ave.
Chicago, Illinois 60660

Dear Carpet People,

Do you have the facilities to dry clean a whale skin?

I have an old whale-hide that is about 60 feet long by 20 feet wide.
I've had it for several years and am ashamed to admit that it has
not always been well looked after. I use it as a throw rug, but in
some places it is more than nine inches thick, which makes it a
little tricky to walk on, especially in high heels. Table legs are
always making permanent indentations, too.

In all these years I've never taken it out to be cleaned, not even
for a good beating over the clothesline. The layer of blubber is
yellowing and I'm afraid the whole thing is really getting to be
an eyesore.

Could you give me some kind of ballpark estimate as to the cost of
cleaning it? By the way, do you think you could also do something
about the cigarette burns?

Look forward to hearing from you.

Sincerely,

W. Stuart Wade

"The Carpet People"
1421 W. Devon Ave.
Chicago, IL 60660

Phone: (312) 743-1300   Fax: (312) 743-1319

1/15/93

Dear Mr or Mrs. Wade,

We are in receipt of your written inquiry regarding cleaning whale skins. To answer your question, yes we can clean that piece. Enclosed you will find a brochure visualizing the various aspects of our business. In addition, we will send you a promotional flyer which we are currently running. Please call 743-1300 and ask for either Mat or Darwin. We are looking forward to hear from you soon.

Regards,

Darwin

W. STUART WADE

3023 N. Clark Street, No. 789
Chicago, Illinois 60657
USA

NO REPLY

August 24th, 1992

Cunard Lines
30-35 Pall Mall
London SW1Y 5LS
England

Dear sirs,

I am quite keen to book a passage on the *Queen Elizabeth II* some-
time within the next twelve to eighteen months. My
preference would be for a round-the-world sailing, but I would also
consider a leisurely trans-Atlantic or trans-Pacific crossing.
I would be travelling together with my Sudanese manservant
Djibui, who of course would require separate quarters.

One very important question which I need to have answered
concerns Djibui's religious practices. As he is of the animist
Ba'Nal faith, I would like to know if he will be allowed to bring
with him the ceremonial vases containing fresh hog entrails which
he uses in his daily prayers. Or by any chance is the *QE2* already
outfitted with them?

If not, it would be necessary for Djibui to post these vases (about
four feet in height) at a few key places around the ship so he has
access to them at all times, and for that reason I wonder if you
would be so kind as to provide me with a layout of the various
decks, etc.

Many thanks in advance for helping us with this most delicate
problem.

Yours sincerely,

W. Stuart Wade

PS. In case you already do have the vases on board for the benefit
of other Ba'Nalist passengers, I'm afraid freeze-dried entrails
have been reclassified in Khartoum as Unorthodox and will
not be acceptable to Djibui.

W. STUART WADE

3023 N. Clark Street, No. 789
Chicago, Illinois 60657

August 11th, 1993

National Photo Archive
Washington, D.C. 20408

Dear sirs,

I read not too long ago that the biggest-selling photo of all time from the commercial sales office of your Archive is the one of President Nixon shaking hands with Elvis Presley. This is not really so surprising when you think about it, because to many people, such a photo must truly define an era in history better than any book or magazine article can

Can you please help me? I am trying to locate similar photographs of other well-known pairs, each of which would also capture the essence of some fleeting moment in a bygone age. Do you have in stock any photos depicting the following people shaking hands, smiling at each other, or in some other way expressing their sense of mutual friendship and admiration:

> Gen. Charles de Gaulle and Jerry Lewis
> Idi Amin Dada and Minnie Ripperton
> Glenn Ford and Pope Pius XII
> Dyan Cannon and Moshe Dayan
> Isaac Asimov and Sting
> Shirley MacLaine and Edgar Allen Poe

This next one will be difficult, but have you got a group shot depicting that crying Indian in the '60's TV pollution ad together with the cast of "Leave it to Beaver"?

Please let me know if these (or any other suitable combinations - please use your judgement) are available, and at what price.

Yours sincerely,

W. Stuart Wade

155

W. STUART WADE

3023 N. Clark Street, No. 789
Chicago, Illinois 60657

September 7th, 1992

Norma's Jeans
4400 E-W Highway, No. 314P
Bethesda, Maryland 20814

Dear sirs,

Your ad in the movie magazine *Premiere* interested me, because
I have been a keen collector of movie memorabilia for more
than twenty years. My collection is not very big, but (without want-
ing to brag) I think it represents a fascinating cross-section
of cinematic history.

My favorite piece in the whole collection is the first acquisition
I ever made. I was on a business trip to Salzburg, Austria, and managed to find the time one evening to locate the famous gazebo
from "The Sound of Music" and saw off a two-by-four.

Would you happen to know where I can find the Pamper Ben
Kingsley wore in "Gandhi"? I am prepared to shell out very big
bucks for it.

Thank you very much in advance for any help you can give me.

Yours sincerely,

W. Stuart Wade

W. STUART WADE

3023 N. Clark Street, No. 789
Chicago, Illinois 60657

September 29th, 1992

Bristol Myers Co.
Attn. Children's Vitamin Brand Manager
345 Park Avenue
New York, New York 10154

Dear sir or madam:

How long has it been since vitamin tablets have been manufactured to resemble well-known cartoon characters? Does this really make youngsters more interested in eating them?

I would like to suggest an educational alternative. Instead of the Flintstones and other fictional characters whose influence on children is not truly meaningful (unless you feel strongly that they learn how to yell "Yabba-dabba-do"), I propose that you launch a brand of vitamins in the shape of busts of Great Figures in History. Thus the vitamins could enrich body and mind.

Below I have outlined a sample program for you.

Strawberry	Orange	Lemon	Banana
Teddy Roosevelt	Sun Yat-sen	Haile Selassie	Socrates
Marie Curie	Martin Luther	David Lloyd George	Simon Bolivar
Napoleon Bonaparte	Thomas Edison	Albert Einstein	Morley Safer*
William Tell	Mahatma Gandhi	Gregory Peck	James Joyce
Thomas Aquinas	Buzz Aldrin*	Ponce de Leon	Abraham Lincoln
Wolfgang A. Mozart	Michelangelo	Orville Wright	Bob Knight

I would be very interested in your reaction to this marketing idea, which is certainly feasible from a technical point of view. After all, if it is possible to make a Barney Rubble vitamin, you could surely make one shaped like Moses or Albert Schweitzer. Please be aware that I have no financial interest in it myself; I only want to do what is best for the children of this country.

Sincerely yours,

W. Stuart Wade

*Just some personal favorites; possibly you would have others in mind.

JAMES C. WADE III

P.O. Box 103
Montchoisi
1000 Lausanne 19, Switzerland

NO REPLY

August 23rd, 1993

Philip Morris Companies, Inc.
Attn: Product Manager, Jell-O
120 Park Avenue
New York, New York USA 10017

Dear sir or madam,

You have been enormously successful over the years in getting American homes to stock Jell-O on their shelves. But what about eating the stuff? If you want your sales to go up, you've got to find ways to get people to eat up the Jell-O they have at home, and go out and buy more. It's no good to you if they buy some and keep it in the cupboard for six months.

To achieve this, I would like to propose that you launch a newsletter full of feature articles that keep people interested in - even talking about - Jell-O. Called *Jell-O-Mail*, it would be sent free of charge to every household in America every month (later on you could charge for subscriptions).

To make *Jell-O-Mail* the best publication of its kind on the market, it cannot contain recipes and other boring tripe that people glance at and pitch directly in the bin: instead it must have articles that make people see at once how exciting and significant Jell-O is. For example:

- How FDR used Jell-O to win World War II
- Jell-O around the house: 10 new uses (not focusing on anything prurient, of course)
- Erich von Däniken: was the secret of Jell-O brought here by extraterrestrials?
- How Jell-O saved my marriage - Walter Cronkite

There might also be occasional Jell-O-Grams, e.g. whenever Jell-O is in the headlines: in deficit reduction discussions, in Bosnia, and so on.

I would like to offer you my services as European editor and roving reporter. I have become aware that Jell-O is served weekly to at least three crowned heads. I've requested interviews.

I look forward to your thoughts on this project and to our future cooperation.

Sincerely yours,

158

JAMES C. WADE III

P.O. Box 103
Montchoisi
1000 Lausanne 19, Switzerland

November 7th, 1993

Philip Morris Companies, Inc.
Attn: Product Manager, Jell-O
120 Park Avenue
New York, New York 10017
USA

Dear sir or madam,

Did you ever receive my letter of August 23rd? I am still quite
interested in getting you set up with a nationwide publication called
Jell-O-Mail, and I hope you are, too. I have done a quick, back-of-
the-envelope calculation of the costs that would be involved. If my
numbers are correct, I believe you could launch this "organ" for
about $100 million if you don't go hog wild on the 4-color printing.

I have given some thought to the content of your first *Jell-O-Gram*.
What do you say to this:

```
WASHINGTON - HILARY CLINTON TODAY UNVEILED
HER LONG AWAITED LIST OF FOODS WHICH WILL BE
REQUIRED EATING UNDER THE ADMINISTRATION'S
NEW HEALTH CARE PACKAGE.  FIGURING AT THE TOP
OF THE LIST WAS JELL-O, THAT DELICIOUS DESSERT
AND/OR SALAD THAT EVERY AMERICAN LOVES.
HOARDING OF JELL-O IS EXPECTED TO CREATE
SEVERE SHORTAGES.
```

Of course, a certain amount of hyperbole is par for the course for
these things. Nevertheless, I hope you like it - and I'm sure it would
work wonders for you.

Looking forward to hearing from you,

Yours,

James Wade

JAMES C. WADE III

P.O. Box 103
Montchoisi
1000 Lausanne 19
Switzerland

NO REPLY

August 23rd, 1993

University of Nebraska
Attn. the Chairman, Dept. of English Literature
Lincoln, Nebraska 68588
USA

Dear sir or madam,

My brother Stuart and I have developed the world's first Karaoke
Shakespeare system, due on the market next year. The orchestral background music establishes a given rhythm, e.g. iambic pentameter, and the
audience participants can then belt out their own soliloquies and dialogues.

The plays available so far are *Julius Caesar, Romeo and Juliet, Hamlet,
Macbeth, Some Like it Hot,* and *The Merry Wives of Windsor.* At present we
are working at breakneck speed on all the rest of Shakespeare's stuff, and
plan to move on to other Eng. Lit. mega-stars as soon as we can. We have
heard rumors that Sony is working on a complete set of Karaoke Milton,
so the competition is bound to heat up soon. Next in the roll-out, we
have our eye on Marlowe and John Donne.

The reason I am writing is to ask whether you would give us your endorsement. We already plan to use the following two endorsements on the kit's
package:

"Really brings the Bard to life! We had a *#@%?! blast!"
—Harvard University

"At last, a chance for everyone to perform Shakespeare's enduring
classics....We can hardly wait for Beowulf!" —Oxford University

Stuart and I would be very grateful if you could add an endorsement as well.
We would particularly appreciate having a good word from a big state university like Nebraska, as we do not want potential buyers to think that our
system is only for the Harvards and Oxfords of the world. I'm sure you
understand what we mean.

Looking forward to your reply,

Sincerely yours,

160

JAMES C. WADE III

P.O. Box 103
Montchoisi
1000 Lausanne 19
Switzerland

December 27th, 1992

Miss Diana Ross
P.O. Box 1683
New York NY 10185
USA

Dear Miss Ross,

On Christmas Day I composed a song in your honor and would be so
happy if you would consider recording it. I wrote it especially for your
voice, which I have loved and thrilled to since your early Motown days.
(By the way, is it possible you are also a ham radio operator?)

Anyway, here is the song. I really hope you like it. Unfortunately, I am not
able to read or write music, but the tune is pretty simple. It goes like this:

> Duh-duh-dee-dum-dee-dum-dum, duh-duh-dee-dum-de-
> dum-deedly-dum-dah,
> dum-dum-dee-dum-doo-doodly, dum-dum-deedoodly-
> doodly-dee.

The second verse is the same as the first, and then the refrain
goes like this:

> Oh, dum-dee dee, oh, dum-dee-dee-DAH! Dee-doo-dahdiddly-
> oh, oh, dum-doo-diddly-oh-dah, wah wah!

As for the lyrics, I believe they should be about sunshine or possibly life
on a farm. Maybe you could suggest a good lyric writer, as that side of the
business is frankly not my forte. If you want to make it a "big city" song,
that's OK, too. I understand that maybe farm life is not up your alley.

I sincerely hope you like this song and would be very happy to hear from
you soon.

Yours sincerely,

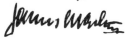

161

W. STUART WADE

3023 N. Clark Street, No. 789
Chicago, Illinois 60657

August 11th, 1992

Nordic Trak
141 Jonathon Boulevard North
Chaska, Minnesota 55318

Dear sirs,

Do you have a machine that builds up facial muscles?
Mine are flaccid.

I look forward to your response.

Yours sincerely,

W. Stuart Wade

W. STUART WADE

3023 N. Clark Street, No. 789
Chicago, Illinois 60657
USA

NO REPLY

May 31st, 1994

Ticketmaster
78 St. Martin's Lane
London WC2N 4AA
England

Dear sirs,

Can you arrange for tickets for special events anywhere in the
world? I am unable to find anyone here in Chicago who can help
me with my particular request, and I got your name and address
from a local ticket agency who suggested I give you a try.

I recently learned that an old school friend of mine is scheduled to
be beheaded in Saudi Arabia in August, and my wife and I thought
we might go and see him off if we can get good seats. Would you
be able to provide these?

I look forward to hearing from you soon.

Yours sincerely,

W. Stuart Wade

JAMES C. WADE III

P.O. Box 103
Montchoisi
1000 Lausanne 19
Switzerland

May 5th, 1992

Ringling Bros. and Barnum & Bailey Circus
Attn. the Personnel Manager
P.O. Box 1528
Venice, Florida 33595
USA

Dear sir or madam,

Are you on the lookout for new talent for your circus? If so, may I suggest that you consider my sister Norella Wade, who is truly sideshow material. Norella possesses a remarkable ability to drink noxious and even corrosive liquids without doing herself the slightest physical harm. For example, in a typical evening she can drink a pint of nail polish remover, then perhaps a bottle of ink (blue-black is presently her favorite flavor), topped off by a chaser of creme de menthe or mercurochrome, whichever is handy.

Norella has had this talent since she was about nine. One hot summer day, she came into the family kitchen and in one long chug, she downed a large stein of cold cream of mushroom soup. It is a moment I have been unable to forget.

The reason I am suggesting she join you is that Norella has begun to tipple a bit. (Please keep this confidential.) On more than one occasion, I have caught her swigging oven cleaner straight from the bottle. As you can imagine, this has me concerned, and I was thinking that if she were to use her talents for a good cause, for example to entertain people in the circus, it would help keep her on the straight and narrow, if you see what I mean.

We've discussed this, and Norella agrees that sideshow work would be challenging. Unfortunately, she is unable to come to Florida for a job interview at the moment, as she is in the hospital recovering from internal lava burns.

Please let me know what you think of this idea. I am sure she would add a great deal to your already fabulous circus. I look forward to hearing from you soon.

Yours sincerely,

[signature]

164

CONNIE P. KEPPEL
Corporate Human Resource Director

June 2, 1992

Mr. James C. Wade III
P.O. Box 103, Montchoisi
1000 Lausanne 19
Switzerland

Dear Mr. Wade:

    Your very interesting letter of May 5, 1992 has reached my
office. What a unique sister you have, with such an unusual
talent. I am certain you must be genuinely concerned for her
safety, especially "swigging oven cleaner." Goodness gracious it
gives a whole new meaning to the term "spit and polished."

    I might suggest that your sister remain in Switzerland as an
increase in temperature or altitude could cause a tremendous
implosion from spontaneous combustion. My, that could be quite an
awful disaster when you consider how blue black ink and
mercurochrome can stain.

    While Ringling Bros. and Barnum & Bailey certainly is known
worldwide for its talented performers, alas I feel we would be
hard pressed to convince our audience of Norella's actual
consumption of such toxic substances. I do, however, have a cadre
of friends in the personnel business and I would like to suggest
you contact the Human Resource Director at Chrysler Corporation in
Detroit, Michigan. Norella's internal structure would be of
particular interest to their Research and Development people.
Imagine an engine or exterior that could resist corrosive
substances.

    Thank you for your idea. Best wishes to Norella on her
recovery from her lava burns. And remember in the true words of
P.T. Barnum: "May all your days be circus days;" or was it
"There's a sucker born every minute."

    Anyway, keep those ideas coming!

                        Sincerely,

                        Connie P. Keppel
                        Connie P. Keppel

CPK/cjb

8607 WESTWOOD CENTER DRIVE • VIENNA, VIRGINIA 22182 • (703) 448-4114 • FAX (703) 448-4100